THE CONNOISSEUR SERIES
OF BOOKS FOR COLLECTORS

A HISTORY OF
OAK FURNITURE

PLATE I.

COURT CUPBOARD.　　　　DATED 1610.

Victoria and Albert Museum.

THE CONNOISSEUR SERIES OF BOOKS FOR COLLECTORS
EDITED BY C. REGINALD GRUNDY

A HISTORY
OF
OAK FURNITURE

BY

FRED ROE, R.I., A.R.B.C.

(AUTHOR OF "ANCIENT COFFERS AND CUPBOARDS,"
"OLD OAK FURNITURE," "THE ART OF THE
COFFERER," ETC.; JOINT AUTHOR OF "VANISHING
ENGLAND")

ILLUSTRATED WITH DRAWINGS BY THE
AUTHOR, AND FROM PHOTOGRAPHS

PUBLISHED BY
THE CONNOISSEUR, 1, DUKE STREET, ST. JAMES'S, LONDON, S.W.1
MCMXX

PRINTED BY
BEMROSE & SONS LTD
LONDON AND DERBY

CONTENTS

113533

LIST OF PLATES

vi

LIST OF PLATES—*continued*

LIST OF PLATES—*continued*

NOTE.—All furniture figured amongst the illustrations is English unless otherwise described. A few articles in other woods than oak are included on account of the very typical characteristics of their style.

For a photograph of one of the late Sixteenth or early Seventeenth-century Chests, we are indebted to the owner, Mr. Thos. Scales Carter, of Oak House, Ilkley.

PLATE II.

CUPBOARD.   TEMP. HENRY VII.   FROM BURWARTON, SALOP.

Victoria and Albert Museum.

INTRODUCTION

THE elder Mr. Weller once observed that more widows were married than single women, and approximating with this cryptic utterance is the remark which I recently heard, "There's more old furniture existing nowadays than was ever made years ago." When properly unravelled, the latter assertion may be accepted as a truism. Other equally certain but less known facts also exist. Since the increase of publication of well-illustrated books depicting specimens of ancient furniture of unusual interest as regards form or structure, the reduplication of such types with a simulated appearance of age has become an active industry. It is seldom, however, that the copying of such pieces from a pictorial illustration is anything of a real success, and if once placed beside the genuine article the difference in contour and quality would be both obvious and surprising.

Occasionally it has happened that spurious (or mainly spurious) rarities have escaped challenge, and have appeared somehow in illustrated works on the subject of ancient furniture as articles of rare interest. These also, in spite of their ambiguous origin, have not escaped duplication, and the result has been a continuous declension, tending much to mystify the embryo collector with a little knowledge as to styles.

Avowed and open reproduction of furniture on antique lines, manufactured from old beams and timbers reaved from barns and housebreakers' debris, is at the present time carried on with a good deal of ingenuity, and it is not infrequently remarked among the Philistines that such skilful imitations must detract from the value of original pieces. A greater fallacy never existed. Each one of these "faked" reproductions could be successfully refuted by the expert connoisseur, and as a parallel it may be remarked that the modern reproduction of ushabtiu and scarabs by thousands has never deteriorated the value of one single true piece dear to Egyptologists.

The higher flights of forgery in all their various departments have for the last decade or so reached a pitch which it is difficult to define as either fine art or science. To accomplish that which shall successfully deceive the penetration of the cautious expert is a task which requires something more than ingenuity nowadays, and the superficial methods which imposed on human credulity some few years ago are being superseded in favour of systematical approach and a general thoroughness of execution, the result of which it is sometimes exceedingly hard to unmask. But the difficulty of accomplishing successful detection in a really tough case is infinitely better for sharpening the wits of the collector than the steady and easy acquisition of true specimens of any class of antiquities whatsoever, and the resultant advantages are both lasting and sufficiently obvious.

Forgeries may be roughly separated into two classes: (1) the forgery rank and complete, and (2) the forgery which is a make-up or a composition of old and new artfully combined. Of these two species the latter is by far the most dangerous, being frequently a pretty object-lesson of the "half a lie" which is so hard a matter to fight. On the whole the French forger is more clever at the game than either his English or Belgian prototype. It is a well-accredited fact that the best of the "fakers" in France take the trouble to reproduce the tools of some three or four hundred years ago before proceeding to attack the actual wood in their productions. Wear is not simulated by the use of sand-paper—a very inadequate means, but created by the constant rubbing of greasy cloths on such portions as would be most likely to be affected. I have known of an old soldier, badly in want of work, who was employed by an unscrupulous firm to dust some white powder over his clothes, and, after having seated himself in the reproduction of an elbow chair, and finding out from the marks where most wear was likely to come, to have applied himself to the impairing of such parts with coarse sebaceous plush torn from old carriage linings. But forgeries in a certain respect resemble the deeds of other criminals; the small but infallible incongruity or omission which gives away the most artistic crime is seldom absent, and, once descried, can never be misunderstood. One of the very best counterfeits in old oak, as regards surface, which I have ever seen, was primarily detected by the carver having mixed up details of the thirteenth and late fifteenth centuries (each admirable in their way) in a most impossible manner. It is best not to particularise; this wonderful production may at the present moment be the pet object of some so-called antiquary's collection, and to disillusion the owner would be cruel, besides possibly leading the way to complications.

When discriminating about old furniture, one must never forget that farmhouse pieces were always intended as such; that is to say, they were heavy, substantial, perhaps boldly or roughly-carved specimens made for the yeoman or middle class for which they were originally intended. The well-bred gallants and doubtful ladies of Charles's court, who masqueraded as swains and shepherdesses, were no more the real article than the rugged, carved armchair was the type or mould which was fashionable in more elevated circles. Marie Antoinette playing at haymaking at the Petit Trianon is not to be compared to the woollen-yarned and buskinned bucolics whose veritable labours were mimicked so lightly. And yet, both as a paradox and a parallel, how many descendants of ancient families can be traced into the humblest of surroundings, even as court furniture, through nameless vicissitudes, has often found its abode in the dwelling of both the yeoman and the tenant farmer side by side with the substantial and more coarsely-carved pieces made for that class of the community. But it is not difficult for the connoisseur in process of classification to divide the higher patterns from their more humble prototypes, always remembering to make allowance for an advance in the change of style in the case of court pieces, sometimes as much as over forty years' difference being observable between objects of similar use that were actually made at one and the same time. Other instances are even more discrepant, and a late country-made piece may at first sight exhibit superficially earlier characteristics than its town-made brethren, which can be disproved on close and thorough examination. Such examples are not unfrequently met with. Let us take a few examples and compare them—

(1) A chest of severely architectural design bearing a date about the middle of the sixteenth century. The piece is modelled on classic lines, and unquestionably belongs to the year inscribed on it, but a casual observer would assign it to a date not earlier than the early part of the seventeenth century. An exceedingly courtly and well-designed piece in advance of its time.

(2) A chest from the West Country, of an earlier style than the last, carved with medallions and heads in profile, and, roughly speaking, representative of a certain style that prevailed during the reign of Henry VIII. A date (during the first quarter of the seventeenth century) which is incised upon the top transom has been challenged as an addition made by an owner subsequent to the time when the chest was made, but careful examination discovers a thinness of the uprights and certain peculiarities in costume which undoubtedly place this particular article as belonging to the date which appears on it. Ergo, a countryside piece exhibiting lingering traditions, and behind the times as regards style.

Such curious discrepancies are at first sight rather puzzling, but they belong to a distinctly different class to the anachronisms perpetrated by many modern carvers, and their discovery leaves no shadow of doubt on the veritable piece which exhibits them.

A few of the pitfalls for the unwary have been touched upon here, but for those who run and read as well, the acquirement of antique oak is a pursuit which increases in ardent interest as the quarry grows scarcer.

FRED ROE.

18, STANFORD ROAD,
KENSINGTON COURT, W. 8.

CHAPTER I.

English Furniture.

From the Thirteenth to the End of the Seventeenth Century.

THE history of furniture is in many respects a record of the architectural styles which have prevailed in the country to which such furniture belongs, and without some auxiliary knowledge of architecture it is impossible to develop any sound attainments on the subject of antique furniture. Again, some knowledge of costume is occasionally very helpful in determining the ages of debatable pieces bearing representations of the human figure, though discoveries of these rarities occur only too seldom. As regards early furniture made from wood, it appears as though oak was the sole material used, the softer trees being ignored, or else we must conclude that any articles made from them in Gothic times must have perished. The earliest pieces of furniture constructed were doubtless chairs and coffers, or boxes of some sort, and as these must have been originally intended for hard wear and strength, the tougher material was probably invariably used by choice. As instances of what solid construction combined with heart of oak may effect, a great number of thirteenth-century coffers remain in this country to testify. These receptacles, which exist mainly in churches, were so hardy and indestructible that with the slow increase of the population it was apparently unnecessary to construct but few pieces of a similar kind in the two succeeding centuries, the older coffers remaining in use long after the craftsman who made them had gone to dust. This is the most potent reason I can advance for the numerous examples of thirteenth-century boxes yet existing compared with the very scanty number of such pieces belonging to the two succeeding centuries.

Eliminating archaic relics of pre-Norman origin, it is possible that the earliest coffer remaining in England which is decorated with any carving is that in Hindringham Church, Norfolk. An arcade of interlaced semi-circular arches of the Transition Norman period is incised on the front panel and uprights of this probably unique piece, which can hardly have emanated from a later period than the last quarter of the twelfth century. A coffer in Graveney Church, Kent, which exhibits incised carving of a similarly early kind, follows close upon its heels; but as the arcading in the Graveney example is composed of pointed and cusped arches of the subsequent Early English style, it is obvious that the priority of some years must be given to the Hindringham relic.

Coffers of this period, down to the end of the thirteenth century, were not provided in the ordinary way with hinges, the lids revolving on iron pins which were inserted horizontally through the back uprights, while the rear panels were often protected by chains. It has been conjectured by some, from observing fragments of these chains remaining, that they were attached for the purpose of fastening such

4

PLATE III.

COFFER OF N. FARES.   TEMP. HENRY VII.

Victoria and Albert Museum.

coffers to the wall, but this is a fallacy, as their intention was really the safeguarding of the receptacle from illicit attack by strengthening the connection of the lid with the body. The uprights of these coffers are invariably of great width, and are frequently termed standards. A thirteenth-century coffer of small size exists at Pitstone, Bucks., in which the standards are wider than the central panel.

Thirteenth-century coffers which exhibit elaborate carving or geometrical roundels incised on their fronts exist, among other places, at the churches of Saltwood, Kent; Stoke d'Abernon, Surrey; Earl Stonham, Suffolk; Westminster Abbey, and York Cathedral. Sussex is also particularly rich in thirteenth-century carved coffers, notably those remaining at the churches of Buxted, Clymping, Felpham, Midhurst, South Bersted, and Chichester Cathedral.

Coffers bound with iron scrollwork, and approximating to the same period, may be found in a fair amount of English churches, those at Brampton, Northants; Chobham, Surrey; Icklingham, Suffolk; Salton, Yorks.; and Wootton-Wawen and Rugby, Warwickshire, being among the most notable. The last-mentioned example is mounted on wooden wheels for purposes of transport.

English coffers belonging to the fourteenth century are much scarcer than the foregoing, but beautifully carved specimens remain at Brailes, Warwickshire; Dersingham and South Acre, Norfolk; All Saints' Church, Hereford; Litcham, Norfolk; and St. John's Hospital, Canterbury. Other fine patterns of this period may also be found, but in many cases they have been mutilated by wilful and ignorant persons. Lincolnshire, perhaps, possesses two of the most complete fourteenth-century relics of this class in the coffer at Haconby Church and the chest at Huttoft. I use the words "coffer" and "chest" in the strictly architectural term, as applied to boxes composed of single panels, as compared with those constructed with multiplied framing. Most of the examples mentioned exhibit the winding tracery peculiar to the Decorated style—a continuous flow of curvilinear lines which trail into each other without the stops and uprights inaugurated by the succeeding Perpendicular method. Chairs or benches of the thirteenth and fourteenth centuries, belonging to anything else than church furniture, hardly exist in England, and those which do remain can in nearly every instance be recognised as fragments of stalls; but a few standing cupboards of heavy build continue with us, their doors bearing strap hinges terminating in an ornamental finish. A fine specimen of this description is preserved in Chester Cathedral, and may be accepted as the type of cupboard generally in use among the better classes during the thirteenth and fourteenth centuries.

English coffers of the fifteenth century are even rarer than those of the preceding epoch. A few iron-bound receptacles belonging to the period exist, but those bearing any representation of the tracery of the period are scant enough. The churches of Barrow-on-Soar, Leicestershire; St. Michael's, Coventry; and perhaps Little Waldingfield, Suffolk, furnish the most notable examples. Flemish chests, such as those of St. Mary's Church, Cambridge, or Southwold, Suffolk, may date from this period, but they do not represent the national art and craft which we are considering. Some hutches and cupboards pierced with late Perpendicular tracery have been discovered during recent years, but these are food receptacles, mostly of rough make, and from their decoration belong to the borderland of the fifteenth and the succeeding century.

During the reign of Henry VII. furniture began to make a distinct advance, both as regards design and construction. That we were later in our developments than most European countries there is no doubt whatever, but it is also quite certain that we preserved a good many of our national characteristics, even throughout the changes effected by the Renaissance. Material was lavishly employed in our home-made productions, and the bold cutting of the English craftsman was distinct from the florid heaviness of the German, or the finely-traceried productions of the French. Flemish work affected us, but during the declining Gothic style its bias was rarely felt inside the East Coast, and was evanescent. In the style which is coeval with the first half of the sixteenth century, the Flemings asserted themselves more fully, and were much patronised in Court circles and by the wealthy for their products; but their mode was not really an original one, consisting as it did of the borrowed revival of Italy affected by their own somewhat ponderous temperament. Abundant proof that the Flemings were more successful here in their quasi-Roman productions than in their earlier style may be found in the evidences of their hands, which exist all over the country in the shape of screens and fixed woodwork generally.

We get the earliest distinct evidences of English domestic furniture in pieces belonging to the reign of Henry VII., which have existed down to the present time, and on these we may find Gothic tracery of a debased type, insidious suggestions of Italian detail, and the linen panel.* Such decorations, however, run more abundantly through the succeeding reign, and it must not be assumed, if any of these characteristics appear in conjunction with each other, that the piece bearing them must necessarily belong to the first Tudor's reign. Only discrimination will determine that, and even then but rarely. It is likely that the greater portion of the furniture made for domestic purposes was cumbrous and unadorned with carving, and that it was broken up for the sake of the material when newer modes came in. Feudal customs had not yet departed, and huge trestle-tables with independent tops were still in use in the halls of the great, while forms and benches constituted the major part of the seating accommodation, only those personages on the daïs being provided with chairs.

Side-tables and credences were more elaborate, and the best pieces presented an effect in which exquisite design is tempered with restraint. Such examples are extremely rare, but our Victoria and Albert Museum possesses a specimen of English art of the end of the fifteenth century which it would be difficult to excel.† This is an oak side-table of somewhat low dimensions, having a shallow cupboard beneath, and its front panels perforated with devices, among which appear the sacred initials "I.H.S." surmounted with a crown, the arms of FRANCE MODERN, the Tudor

---

* Portrait heads in profile were not enclosed in roundels till the reign of Henry VIII., when the Renaissance was established.

† No. W. 47—1910.

rose, and a window of late Gothic tracery. In the sides are linen panels placed longitudinally, and the space for a door, which is now missing, appears in the centre of the cupboard beneath the table. This beautiful and interesting piece was evidently made for some personage of high rank, and was probably used for the carving of food and its temporary holding.

A few chairs and stools of the same period are left to us. One very perfect linen-panelled specimen is at St. Dònat's Castle, in the collection formed by the late Mr. Morgan Williams, while an excellent range of slab-ended stools of the keyed type has been gathered together within recent years by the Marquess of Granby. Of the subsequently developed pattern of "joyned," or joint stools, Sir George Donaldson possesses some remarkable examples.

In 1909 great interest was aroused by an announcement which was made in the daily papers that His Majesty (the late King Edward VII.) would use in one of his levees an historic oak chair, an heirloom of a Warwickshire family, and which was traditionally supposed to have been used by Henry Tudor, Earl of Richmond, afterwards King Henry VII., at a council of war held on August 20th, 1485, at the Three Tuns Inn, Atherstone, where he spent the night. How the chair came into the possession of the family is not quite certain, but it is supposed to have been purchased some three generations ago, when the said inn was pulled down. That the chair was an old one there was no doubt about, but on the publication of a photograph it at once became apparent that the chair for which so interesting a history was claimed could not possibly be older than the seventeenth century. The back was panelled and carved with an arch enclosing a diamond, in true Jacobean style, and the turned legs were utterly unlike anything imagined or executed by craftsmen of the time of Henry VII. This incident will be fairly fresh in the minds of students of early furniture.

A supposition attached to an oak cupboard in the Victoria and Albert Museum has more possibility about it. This piece, which is a tall standing press of rough construction, is fashioned in the flat shape associated with the reigns of the two last Henrys. It is, by the way, wrongly described as a "Livery Cupboard," and is supposed by some to be connected with Prince Arthur, eldest son of Henry VII., who died in 1502, in his sixteenth year. The front of this cupboard exhibits a number of carved rosettes and wheels, and the doors to its two stages are placed in the centre, as was invariably the case about this period. The top door and its attendant side panels are pierced with windows exhibiting Gothic tracery of a late type, that in the door being pointed, and those in the panels being flat topped. There is absolutely nothing about the cupboard to suggest that it belongs to any other period than the epoch named, and it is equally certain that it is of English make; but the attribution of its ownership, which is based on certain decorations, hardly proves conclusive. Right and left of the door on the lower stage appear certain perforated decorations, which, it is asserted, represent the ostrich feathers appertaining to the Prince of Wales. The matter is quite a debatable one, and depends in great measure as to the real meaning of these devices. For my own part,

I am not sufficiently impressed with the hypothesis of its princely attribution, which has the disadvantage of being open to some grave objections, too lengthy to be discussed here. This press is an exceptionally interesting piece, and the accuracy or otherwise of the foregoing legend makes no difference to its antiquarian value; but it is doubtful whether such a roughly-made article would be built for so high a personage as Prince Arthur, and with all reservation I must state my belief that the devices represent in some way a rebus on the name of the original owner, or an intimation as to his calling or pursuits.*

Another domestic piece of the same period in the Museum is an oak coffer, carved on its obverse with the conventional rose-bush and flowering, and on the reverse with a vine-trail and the inscription " N. FARES," accompanied by an object which looks suspiciously like a skull-cap. The reverse side is flanked with buttresses, and on one end alone appears the monogram "N.F.," surmounted by a similar skull-cap. The lid is very massive and weighty, and bears on its fore edge a beautiful Gothic moulding. To my mind this intensely attractive piece must have been the business coffer of some leech or apothecary of high standing. The end destitute of carving would be placed against the wall, and on the opening side of the coffer (which would also serve as a counter) Mr. Fares would sit to dispense his prescriptions, while on the other (that adorned with buttresses) his patients would be continually reminded of his honoured name. The carved monogram on the side would be visible to those who passed the counter into the inner sanctum for a private consultation. This unique piece was formerly elevated on legs, and a canopy of depressed Gothic arches appears between the buttresses on the side which would face the public, as well as a single arch beneath the monogram on its carved ends. No arches were placed on the side which Mr. Fares would sit at, the omission being obviously for comfort in accommodating his knees beneath the body of the coffer. I know of no domestic piece which possesses a deeper interest in suggesting a history of its primary uses.

It is curious that the early cabinet-makers should have had so little of the utilitarian about them that they persisted in placing the small doors of their cupboards invariably in the centre of the piece, an inconvenient arrangement, which allowed the users to grope about blindly in corners, with but remote chance of finding what they required. English cupboards of late fifteenth and early sixteenth century design were without prominences and wanting in contour, for, while assimilating the features of the Renaissance, the bold ornate outlines of the Italian cassones did not seem to have been followed by our English craftsmen. Cornice mouldings were flat, stiles were wide, and panels often unnecessarily small. We occasionally find cupboards and chests of the time of Henry VIII., the plain contour of whose fronts is broken by heads in high relief, boldly projecting from the centre of the panelling, but it was not till the age of Elizabeth that any leaning was shown towards

---

* No. W. 15—1912, Victoria and Albert Museum. Presented by Robert Mond, Esq., F.S.A., through the National Art Collections Fund.

canopied recesses and baluster supports. The forms of decoration employed in England during the first half of the sixteenth century were arabesques, pilasters, and grotesque heads enclosed in roundels. Henry VIII. greatly encouraged foreign craftsmen, and there is no doubt that much of the woodwork executed here in his time was carved by Flemings, Germans, and Italians. A few of the English craftsmen persisted in their endeavours to perpetuate the moribund Gothic style, such efforts being, properly speaking, a species of dogged defence or inability to assimilate more fashionable modes, which was peculiar to our own country alone. Some curious instances of such contrarieties are noted in the chapter on "Furniture Bearing Dates."

Large tables and forms were seldom decorated with carving in our own country about the time of Henry VIII., such æsthetic qualities as they possessed being afforded by the outline alone. The quaint early custom of having connecting tie-bars running underneath the centre of the table instead of foot-rails, and keyed at each end by means of wedges, was adhered to in great measure, and most of these tables, which are classed as "Gothic," belong really to a period subsequent to the age which they are supposed to represent.

Small occasional tables for the purpose of playing at cards and other games were, unlike their larger brethren, highly enriched with carving. Shaw gives a very careful engraving of one of these in his book on "Ancient Furniture," and mentions it as being in the possession of Mr. Swaby "from Hill Hall, Essex."* A table similar to the foregoing was exhibited at the Franco-British Exhibition in 1908, and was so remarkably like the specimen in Shaw's book that I am tempted to think it may be one and the same, though without having had an opportunity of closely examining it. If not the identical specimen, it at least must be from the hand of the same craftsman. A chair of precisely the same period, and decorated with roundels and ornaments of exactly the same character, is also figured in Shaw's work, the following description being attached to it:—"Chair of the time of Henry the Eighth, in the possession of Joseph Abel, Esq., Surgeon, Mitchel Dean, Gloucestershire. This interesting example is of a period after the introduction of what was termed 'Romayne work' into England; that is, when the frescoes adopted by Raphael and other celebrated painters from the antique had given a new character to ornamental furniture. It is so carved within, and with napkin panelling without, is of oak, and in a good state of preservation."

Writing-desks with slanting lids do not appear to have come into use till after the mid-century was passed; that is, desks which were constructed so as to be movable and not fixed like lecterns. The earliest decorated pattern I can point to in one of these movable desks is in the possession of T. C. Parker, Esq., of Skirwith Abbey, Cumberland. It was picked up in a Westmoreland village, and was supposed to have been originally in the parish church. This piece, which is carved with vine tendrils and thistles, also exhibits profile masks on its sides, the vine-scrolls issuing

---

* *Specimens of Ancient Furniture*, by Henry Shaw, F.S.A. 1836. See plate 28.

from the mouths of the masks.   The piece is decidedly unusual, and I should hesitate to place a later date on it than the first ten years of Elizabeth's reign.

It is difficult to assign any furniture particularly to the reigns of Edward VI. and Mary; their respective reigns—six and five years—were too short to admit of any specialisation.   The wooden arcaded superstructure on Edward the Confessor's shrine in Westminster Abbey, attributed to the reign of Mary, is a somewhat severe piece of classic, which differs essentially from the grotesque vagaries produced in her successors' days.   I have seen at least one piece of furniture bearing an inscription attributing its origin to the reign of the last Tudor king, but I should be somewhat chary of pronouncing upon the genuineness of either inscription or the article itself.

The art of inlaying with different-coloured woods became fashionable during the sixteenth century.   This form of embellishment emanated from Italy, and, spreading through France and Germany, speedily became very much in favour.   It is not unusual to find the inlaid decoration on German chests so closely resemble that on our home-made pieces that it is difficult to believe the work could not be executed by the very same craftsmen.   In most cases, however, the German article will be found to antedate the English, however closely their respective inlay may approximate.   During the latter half of the sixteenth century conventional floral decoration was much in vogue with the inlayers, but the simulation of quartered panels and geometrical insertions was also carried out.   Painting and gilding was also resorted to, though not so freely as in the Gothic times.   An item in the Kenilworth Inventory, taken in 1584, mentions "a bedstead of walnut tree, toppe fashion, the pillars redd and varnished"; and a few articles are still occasionally found which exhibit traces of their embellishments in colour, though this has mostly disappeared under the efforts of the owners to promote a rich polished surface.

Carved terminal figures were first introduced into English furniture during the third quarter of the sixteenth century, on the stiles of chests, cupboards, and the backs of bedsteads.   These figures, far from being of a classic nature, as in Italian specimens, were frequently uncouth, and represented as wearing barbaric head-dresses.   Cupboards assumed greater variety of contour, and were in part recessed, or had their sides facetted in a manner peculiar to productions of the English nation.

Tables of Elizabeth's reign were made in a variety of forms, occasionally being of an architectural character, but more frequently having the legs formed in the shape of huge bulbs decorated with jewel moulding—a complete change to any preceding style.

With the advent of the Stuart dynasty, the history of furniture becomes less complicated.   Classic influences gradually clarified during the later Renaissance, and though many of the mannerisms of Elizabeth's days were primarily adopted, the Jacobean style, on the whole, progressed in purity.   One of the minor exceptions to this as regards surface decoration was in the form of ornament known as strap-work.   Jacobean strap was almost invariably of a more debased shape than that of Elizabeth's time, the terminations often splaying into more or less meaningless forms. Whilst the craze for collecting rare bulbs prevailed in Holland, it was a favourite practice to introduce the tulip into decorative carving. This is an important point to consider since English furniture displaying the tulip can nearly always be assigned to no earlier period than the middle of the seventeenth century. Such articles as chairs, cupboards, and chests remained substantially the same in outline till the Dutch influence introduced in the reign of Charles II. brought a new mode into Court circles. Chests of drawers became more fashionable than chests, being frequently decorated with raised and facetted panels in the Flemish style. With the increase of printing, Bibles became more plentiful, every homestead of any standing possessing a family Bible with its accompanying Bible-box—in reality only a late survival of the coffret. And as feudal customs declined the massive tables which consumed so much of England's ancient oak became replaced by that national product now known as the " gate table." As the Jacobean period progressed, taste verged towards lighter construction. Soft woods in a great measure replaced oak as a material, preparing the way for mahogany in later years. Oak furniture, how-ever, continued to be made in outlying districts well into the eighteenth century, though merely as a decadence of previous types. The one attempt at a definite resurrection of accepted oak styles occurred in the time of Sir Walter Scott, and the result was not altogether a happy one. It is a singular fact that undoubted speci-mens of "Abbotsford" furniture may be seen at the present day in at least one great public collection, being described as dating from the second half of the seventeenth century. It requires little expert training to distinguish these meaningless and heavy attempts at reproduction from the true articles which were produced at the time of Britain's merriest monarch.

CHAPTER II.

ENGLISH OR FOREIGN?

THERE is a distinct disposition among certain present-day collectors and critics to class almost all specimens in England antedating from our Elizabethan style as being of foreign origin, and about this impression there is a good deal to be said. In the first place it is well to enquire what is actually meant by the word "foreign," this appellation being frequently used in such an indiscriminate way that some investigation should fairly be made as to the sense in which it is employed. Does it signify that the piece so referred to was designed abroad, or made abroad, or both designed and made in some country other than England? I have heard dozens of critics who, because they have noticed certain lines and peculiarities in early coffers which exist or have been brought from the Continent, have not hesitated to sweepingly assign an origin French, German, or otherwise to undoubtedly English examples remaining *in situ* in our own country. It is well known that in the thirteenth and early fourteenth centuries certain common characteristics in architecture prevailed more or less over a great part of Europe, and often it is not only difficult, but more than difficult, to "place" an early piece from its actual lines or decorative carving alone. The armoire at Aubazine, in Corrèze, is without doubt a French example, but there is nothing to distinguish it from Anglo-Norman design of the same time, if indeed we possess any so perfect examples of a like date. Again, the coffers at Brancepeth and Wath, indubitably English examples, had rightly never been queried till the recent importation of a German coffer designed on somewhat similar lines raised the hypothetical theory as to their possible origin. The similarity decided the matter in certain quarters, and it was urged by some that the English examples necessarily emanated from a German source. This, however, is hardly conclusive. There are such questions as the nationality of the wood which the pieces are constructed from (German oak differs materially from English), the handling, construction, and several other points which apparently have not been considered. Lastly, but not least, there remains the fact that designs were more freely interchanged during the Middle Ages than is generally imagined, and though sometimes they may not have been adopted in the fullest sense by native families practising their crafts, these designs may have influenced some who would not care to adopt them in their entirety. The English craftsman was often bold and coarse, the German frequently heavy, and it is sometimes a delicate matter to decide authoritatively upon the origin of certain pieces without the most scrupulous examination. The coffer recently acquired by the authorities of the Victoria and Albert Museum (No. V., 49, 1912) bears an extraordinary superficial resemblance to its prototype in Saltwood Church,

12

PLATE IV.

NORTHERN FRENCH COFFER. FIFTEENTH CENTURY.

Victoria and Albert Museum.

Kent; but close scrutiny will discover a certain lumpiness and heaviness of execution very different from the Kentish example. It is well to note that the Kensington coffer came from Cologne, and is stated to have been found in a neighbouring farm-house on the Rhine, also that the material from which it is constructed is German oak.

One thing must be admitted: it is more than singular and worthy of remark that such striking similarities could exist in work produced by different countries in a period so remote as the thirteenth and early fourteenth centuries, while a hundred years later, when communication must necessarily have developed, divergencies in style and character had matured to a remarkable degree. There were few European countries, with the exception of the Scandinavian group, that did not produce directly distinctive types of furniture in the fifteenth century. The variance had by this time become conspicuous. France and Flanders to a certain extent are exceptions to the rule. While it is easy to distinguish between French, German, and English examples of the fifteenth century, it is often a task of some difficulty to differentiate between French and Flemish examples, a slight heaviness in the latter being at times the only observable distinction. In later periods this heaviness became accentuated more fully, and frequently obtrudes itself in an unpleasantly redundant manner. Sir Walter Scott hits off a description of such production rather neatly in the following sentence, quoted from *Paul's Letters to his Kinsfolk*: "The same cumbrous solidity which distinguishes the female figures of Rubens, may be traced in the domestic implements and contrivances of his countrymen."

Similarly, when one examines antique Flemish carvings of human figures, whether statuettes or in relief, we find that the countenances, especially of the women, are portrayed in a stolid, unintellectual cast, Virgin Marys, saints, and mythical characters alike sharing the prevailing ponderosity. The Flemings, as much as any race on earth, adhered to depicting their own immediate types and surroundings, and any lightness or grace which they possessed was most certainly derived from their French neighbours.

One of the most instructive pieces which it would be possible to study in the debatable class is a coffer of carved elm in the Victoria and Albert Museum (W. 30, 1913). This coffer is sculptured on its front with a design of gryphons and scroll-work so unmistakably Tyrolean in character that few would hesitate to pronounce in this wise on its origin from superficial scrutiny. Running round the base, however, appears the confusing inscription:—

BY . JAMES . GRIFFIN
16 . THIS : CHEST . WAS : MAD : IN : THE : YEARE
OF . OUR . 39
LORD : GOD . ANO : DO.

The initials "I.G." also appear in smaller characters in the centre of the front panel. Now here is a piece quite Tyrolean in character, and yet made by a craftsman who obviously worked in our own country, and, eschewing oak, worked in the softer elm for his material. The peculiarities are too strong to admit of any doubt; the flat-surfaced carving is essentially Tyrolese in character, though perhaps the diamond-shaped ornaments scarcely accord; and the very red and black in depressed portions of the carvings is characteristic of the Tyrol. It is, therefore, extremely probable that James Griffin was an immigrant, long resident in England; that the coffer in question was made here for his own family use in the style which he remembered and loved; and also remotely possible that the gryphons (though the device was quite an ordinary one) were intended as a rebus on his name. The material used (elm) must have been selected as being more akin to the consistency of the Alpine fir than our iron-grained national oak. Altogether a very pretty piece of conjectured history.

Another article of furniture in the same museum, but of a very much higher class than the last, is a cabinet of pinewood, elevated on pillared legs, the whole piece being of an architectural design. It is adorned with a number of boxwood carvings in high relief, representing battle scenes, while the flat surfaces are profusely overlaid with designs in marquetry of sycamore, pearwood, Hungarian ash, maple, and other woods. On the base and bordering the inlay appear the rose and portcullis, emblems of the Tudor sovereigns of England. This elaborate piece of furniture, which dates from the middle of the sixteenth century, has nothing in common with English work of that period, and was most probably made by a North Italian craftsman, either for presentation to some personage of high rank in England, or else by his or her order. The front portion of the frieze is capable of being raised, disclosing five secret drawers, which, however, are carved in unison with the rest of the piece.*

---

* No. 27, 1869, Victoria and Albert Museum.

CHAPTER III.

French Furniture.

To the End of the Sixteenth Century.

DESCRIPTIVE syllabus of the various changes that took place in French furniture might well occupy more space than any chapter in this work, so much fancy and originality were exhibited in their various developments. The earlier styles, however, can only be dealt with in the present section, reserving the more recent evolutions for a future dissertation on the subject. As regards the earliest known styles of furniture, pretty much the same may be said of French examples as of their English contemporaries. Both construction and decoration are alike in each case, the singularities being oftentimes strikingly similar. After the thirteenth century, however, changes began to manifest themselves, and by the middle of the fifteenth century, when the Flamboyant style was fully established, the changes between our national productions and those of our French neighbours were very marked. We have little left of our own household movables belonging to this period which can compare with the French for delicacy of carving and precision in the matter of joinery.

In France nowadays the pointed styles are more generally known and appreciated than in England. Not only the middle classes, but the common crowd there are conversant with the style and term "La Gothique" to an extent unknown on this side of the Channel. Our own countrymen, with the exception of the architectural profession and a relatively inconsiderable number of artists and archæologists, are by far the greater part either carelessly indifferent to or else ignorant of the phases of this most beautiful art, and an overwhelming majority even of its actual designation. It is remarkable, too, that among those here who are lovers of the pointed styles of architecture in stone buildings, a comparative few seems to apply the same interest to woodwork of these periods. In England Gothic art is for the few, at least as far as furniture is concerned, and all the transient and, in many cases, misdirected efforts of Walpole, Pugin, Shaw, and Sir Gilbert Scott have not succeeded in re-establishing any wide appreciation of it.

It must not be supposed when one uses the denomination "French" that it is intended to include in one class all periodical similarities from the Pas de Calais to the Pyrenees, or from the Alps to the Côtes du Nord. Provincial differences were just as much varied across the Channel as the discrepancies between our craftsmen of Yorkshire and those of the East Coast, or even more so. Between Norman and Breton work a wide gulf is fixed, and during the latter half of the sixteenth century an even wider divergence existed between the productions of St. Lo and Lyons. This may be partly explained by the resistless push of Italian influence on an art-loving nation such as the French have always been. Italy was conquering with

15

her arts more than with her armies. Yet the best workmanship must greatly depend upon the various styles which periodically reigned in separate provinces. Personally, I am of opinion that though the finest specimens of Gothic may have been produced about Rouen, a chaster and purer classic emanated from towns such as Lyons, Nismes, or other places in the Rhone Valley, where the old Roman influence was yet strong, and where the tide of Italian invasion was more speedily and strongly felt.

At present our attention is on an earlier style—that Gothic which gave Rouen the famous rose-window in its west front, and the church of St. Ouen in all its completeness of style. French furniture of the fourteenth century is scarce enough, like its English prototypes, but of the following epoch there are plenty of examples. While English productions of the fifteenth century are infrequently met with, and in any condition may be regarded as rarities, there is no lack of French household movables of this epoch, they being mostly decorated with the graceful Flamboyant carving which attained to such a pitch in the fifteenth century. Our own local museums seldom enough make any show of antique furniture, but each little dusty public collection of curiosities in provincial France almost invariably contains some treasures in this way, and amongst them a Flamboyant chest is rarely wanting. Eliminating the suspicion that the disastrous effects of the British climate may in some part account for this discrepancy, there can be little doubt that at this period the French nation was more prolific and luxurious than the English. In spite of the destruction caused by time and vandal's hand, modern France, both as to private collections and public museums, teems with chests, chairs, and other articles approximating from the period of Louis XI., contrasting very forcibly with our own scanty relics of the same type and period. French framed chests were more elaborate in their joinery and adornments than the English. The locks were often marvels of intricate workmanship, and throughout almost the whole ran the sinuous convolutions of the Flamboyant style, assisted by the linen panel. The French exhibited intersecting mouldings on the edges of framework (as reverted to elsewhere in this work), also a slight arching over the panels, seldom seen in English furniture of this age. The tracery, too, which adorns French woodwork of the Flamboyant period, is often embellished with a curious diamond-shaped ornament, which, singularly enough, does not seem to have been employed in their stone carvings, and which may be looked for in vain on any of our own national productions.

French chests were more frequently buttressed than those made on this side of the Channel, where a great many receptacles reverted to the simple " coffer " or single-panel type. These buttresses were sometimes adorned with " paned " and spiral carvings of a very elegant description, into which presently began to creep the leafage of the superseding styles.

A good many oak chairs of late fifteenth-century workmanship remain in France, most of them being intended for state occasions, and some very magnificent specimens may be seen in the French museums, adorned with buttresses, and carved on the panels with designs in the Flamboyant style. In Rouen Museum an arm-chair is preserved which is small and of a somewhat more unassuming type, but which has the back perforated with late Flamboyant tracery. The type is a very uncommon one, and details are not wanting that indicate it to be a product of the Transition period at the junction of the centuries. The little dainty Gothic stool from Normandy now in our Victoria and Albert Museum is well known, and is a gem of its kind.* Its lines should be compared with the English specimens of approximately the same date, shown in Plates XXVI., XXVII., and XXVIII., and with the slightly later Italian example in the Victoria and Albert Museum.†

The first breath of the Renaissance did not immediately revolutionise all the features of the late pointed style. Scores and hundreds of pieces exist which exhibit the distinctive peculiarities of the two epochs side by side with each other. The Cluny galleries possess many such specimens, where the synthesis, far from being inconsistent, presents a most pleasing and harmonious appearance. The Gothic died hard, and for a time it actually seemed uncertain which style would absorb the other. But the cult of classic pilasters, foliated scrolls, arabesques, caryatides, and profile masks eventually prevailed, and the Gothic went down, never to recover itself, though a rugged survival existed in Brittany till well into the seventeenth century.

At first the old form of outline was adhered to in furniture as in ecclesiastical buildings; armoires and credences underwent no change in structure, though what may be termed the "trimmings" differed considerably. One has only to look at a multitude of French churches, built or added to about the Transition period, to understand how difficult it was for the old designers to start their reformation of style on anything more elementary than the frills. To mention only a few examples, the churches of St. Eustache, in Paris, commenced in 1532; St. Jacques, Dieppe, built in the sixteenth century; the chapels surrounding the choir of St. Pierre, added in 1521; and the remarkable oak screen to a chapel on the north side of the choir at Evreux Cathedral, may suffice. In each of these exemplifications the prevailing outline is arranged upon Gothic principles, while the details in character belong essentially to the Italian Renaissance. Theoretically, such anomalies are not only wrong, but in very bad taste, yet the *ensemble* is generally rich, and the adaptation shows great inventive faculty.

During the second half of the fifteenth and throughout the following century walnut-wood was much used by the French in the manufacture of furniture. Walnut is of a finer and smoother grain than oak, and is very desirable material for the working of small and intricate details by the carver. Where sap-wood occurs, it is peculiarly liable to the attacks of the worm and decay consequent upon exposure to damp, but where the tree is sound, and pieces worked from such portions are properly kept, walnut will often retain its sharpness to a wonderful degree. It is no unusual thing to see French cabinets and chests made of walnut in which sections are so rotten as to be positively devoid of outline or detail, while adjacent surfaces remain uninjured and exhibit their pristine cutting as clearly as the scoop-marks on a Gruyere cheese.

---

* Normandy oak stool. No. 968, 1897.
† Italian walnut stool, given by Lady Mond. No. W. 10, 1910.

C

Numerous examples of pseudo-classic productions may be seen in the Cluny, Orleans, and other museums; and, while studying the complete examples comprised in these collections, I have been forcibly struck with one thing—in furniture of the Gothic type the French, so far as beauty of outline was concerned, were able to hold their own with any country in the world, but when it came to their merely adopting Italian influence, pieces from the southern country were more subtle and exquisite as far as contour is concerned, be the carving what it may. If two similar pieces of furniture of the Southern French and Italian Renaissance respectively, and *quasi* equal merit as regards execution, be closely compared together, perhaps no superficial superiority may be observed in either article; but view such pieces from a short distance, merely as a mass of contour, and the more refined outlines of the Italian production almost invariably assert themselves.

About 1560 French furniture had assumed a floridity which was often over-elaborated, and which, though the sculpture was frequently highly finished, failed to satisfy as in their Italian prototypes. French design was apt to be overdone and unrestful after the middle of the century was passed, and even in the most superb productions of French craftsmen one often sighs for the introduction of a plain surface to contrast with and accentuate the lavish carving in high relief. Even the very elaborate and well-modelled walnut buffet, or sideboard, from the Soulages collection, now in the South Kensington Museum, shows a want of restraint, while its outline leaves much to be desired. This curious elaboration may be mainly traced to the influence of Jean Gougon, called the " French Phidias," and his attempts to establish a national school of sculpture and design. Gougon appears to have been born in 1515, when the Early Renaissance was in full swing, and we first hear of him as being engaged in embellishing and beautifying the cathedral of Rouen and the church of St. Maclou; grafting, in fact, on an older mode. Though his art was in a way founded on classic models, he in great measure discarded the Italian style and adopted an original treatment quite his own. He was employed by Henri II., and executed a vast amount of pediments, statues, and decorations, among his chief efforts being bas-reliefs upon the Hotel de Carnavalet, the Fontaine des Innocents, and a portion of the façade of the Louvre. Jean Gougon was suspected of being a Huguenot, and tradition has it that he was shot during the massacre of St. Bartholomew while engaged at work in the last-mentioned building. This oral legend, which is an exceedingly old and persistent one, has been controverted with some success; but, at all events, we hear no more of Jean Gougon, and his influence gradually declined. The carvings upon French cabinets and chests of Gougon's time, both in high relief, were frequently executed with much delicacy, but the accompanying mouldings were heavy, and surfaces were clogged with an excess of ornament. Yet, with all its defects, this type of art is distinctly a national one, and deserves full recognition as a movement which proceeded from within. The decline of Gougon's influence in the last quarter of the sixteenth century marked a change in the style of furniture, the subject of which must be reserved for a future occasion.

PLATE V.

NORMANDY STOOL.   FIFTEENTH CENTURY.   VICTORIA AND ALBERT MUSEUM.

CHAPTER IV.

FURNITURE OF THE NETHERLANDS.

THE quantity of oak furniture which sprung from Holland in bygone times is a matter for wonder, but the majority of pieces which we are acquainted with date no earlier than the seventeenth century. Old oak furniture of that period is even now not unplentiful in the market—that is, except in Holland itself, where the greater part of the so-called antiques on sale are fabrications, many of them made and exploited by Frenchmen. The oak tree does not flourish in Holland, and therefore must have been brought down the Rhine from Germany in vast quantities for consumption in the land of bulbs and willows. The oak Dutch furniture is of a very fine grain, the medullary rays not being very distinctly marked. It is softer in substance than English oak, and is capable of being worked by the carver to a high degree of finish. Practically very little remains of Dutch furniture of any period preceding the Renaissance, but from what we know the natives of Holland, unlike their Flemish neighbours, did not take very kindly to Gothic forms in the arts. The custom of painting their furniture with floral emblems was lavishly carried out by the Dutch during the sixteenth and seventeenth centuries, but the effect produced by such embellishment was gaudy, and during the period of its first freshness must have been horribly distracting. The art is said to have been last practised at the little village of Hindeloopen, and to have finally died out during the nineteenth century. The old Dutch Masters were proverbially so faithful in their renderings of contemporary life, that we can study their pictures with the greatest profit when determining the shapes and peculiarities in their furniture. In an oil-painting of high finish by Gerrita Berck-Heyde, representing the interior of the church of St. Bavon, at Haarlem, and dated 1673, we may see a fine large specimen of an early sixteenth-century church coffer, possessing a plurality of locks. This coffer, which is painted a red colour, stands upon clamped feet.

A Dutch or Flemish coffer, boldly carved with figures, is in the South Kensington Museum, the subject on its front panel representing Esther and King Ahasuerus, and bearing this inscription:—

"DE SICK GADES VOLCK VMME THO BRINGEN HADDE VOR GENAMEN ISTOM LESTEN SVIV."

The figures measure some six inches each in height, and their costume shows here and there indications of modes of the sixteenth century, to which period the piece doubtless belongs. Portions of this coffer have been replaced, though it

19

is probably in its original shape. The uprights are richly carved with pilasters and swags, and the whole effect is heavy.

As a type of florid Dutch woodwork of the period, the ornate and yet refined choir-screen at Monnikendam Church, dating from 1562-63, should be studied with much greater advantage. Generally speaking, the outlines and projections of Dutch furniture are bold, while carved decoration, apart from figures, is executed in low relief, scrolls and arabesques being rendered in a manner distinct from those of any other nationality. During the period of the Dutch Renaissance, the doors of cabinets and presses mostly revolved on pin hinges, placed vertically, thus being invisible, and playing no part in the decoration of such pieces. One extremely probable reason that so few pieces of Dutch furniture remain of any date prior to the seventeenth century is the long and destructive struggle which was carried on against the Spaniards under Alva, and the devastation which was caused in this small but obstinate and intrepid country. No people have ever shown themselves fonder of inscribing the dates of erection upon their dwellings than the Dutch, a great number of houses yet remaining in Gronengen, Maastricht, Dordrecht, Delft, and other places which bear sixteenth-century dates, ranging from 1509 to 1571. This custom was doubtless carried out also with regard to specimens of furniture, which, if they had remained in existence, would have afforded an invaluable guide at the present day. We know that after the "Spanish fury" had spent itself, and the deposition of Philip II. had been accompanied by the appointment of William the Silent as Prince of Holland and Zeeland in 1581, the departing Spaniards left many traces of their occupation behind them; leather-backed and seated chairs, inlaid cabinets, and *hispains*, or window casements closed with shutters doubly-hinged, as well as other details, remained to show how deeply the southern race had left their mark upon the domestic life of the nation.

With Dutch oak chairs of the seventeenth century we frequently find that the material employed was not so lavishly used as in English examples, and, contrary to the custom obtained in cabinets and cupboards, the leg and stretcher members are flatter and more restricted as to variety of outline. Table legs, however, exhibited enormous bulbs, though, contrary to the English custom, such bulbs were seldom decorated with carving other than a sunk band or a ridge passing round them.

Cupboards often possessed very wide cornice mouldings, underneath which appeared an elaborately carved frieze, while the façades were supported by pilasters, the upper shafts of which were frequently ebonised, the lower portions, or "drums," being carved in ordinary oak. The doors were sometimes embellished with depressed arches, but more often exhibited small square panels, surrounded by wide mouldings, and bearing in their centre quasi-classic patterns very different from our English strap-work. A brother brush who visited Hoorn between forty and fifty years ago informs me that on market-day there he has seen on the "Plein," among the objects exposed for sale, numerous oak cupboards and presses of the seventeenth century, each one of which would have served as an example for students of design. All of these have now disappeared. Holland is swept clean, though a systematic trade is still carried on in some places (notably at Marken), where the cottages are restocked again and again for the benefit of those visitors who wish to purchase souvenirs of the aborigines.

Towards the end of the seventeenth century cupboards and coffers became heavy and lifeless in design. Such pieces are wanting in the fine lines which we usually associate with the Dutch Renaissance, and possess little attraction for the connoisseur.

A great part of Flanders suffered under the same infliction of the "Spanish fury" which scourged the sister country, but resistance was less successful, and it may be that destruction was not so complete. At all events, we had till lately no lack of old Flemish furniture remaining of every date from the Gothic decline downwards.

Difficulty is often experienced in discriminating French traceried chests from similar productions made by Flemish hands, though the former examples are generally superior and more satisfying to the connoisseur of old oak. The flamboyant style was as popular in Flanders as it was in France, and many contemporary details were identical in these two countries which will never be found in English work, notably the intersection of mouldings, which is referred to in another part of this work, and the rounded-top framing over panels of late Gothic design. But Flemish work, to me at least, has often a somewhat disappointing effect, producing the same sort of feeling which one has on viewing the west front of Brussels Cathedral after lingering over the same aspects in matchless Amiens or Notre Dame de Paris. Not that this simile in any way refers to their respective dates. A fair number of "Flanders chests" still remains in our own country to attest the export industry of the Flemings during the second half of the fifteenth century.

When the Renaissance had taken root, the Flemings seemed to apply themselves with extraordinary vigour to the production of florid specimens of the new style, and a vast quantity of productions, dating from the sixteenth and seventeenth centuries, exist, in which its peculiar features are pushed to their utmost limits. If heads carved on French and English woodwork verged upon the grotesque, those yielded by the Flemish were even more so. A species of heaviness, too, hung about their representations of the human figure, which is consistent with the powerful frames but somewhat sluggish temperament of the people themselves. Mouldings did not escape this ponderousness, and many a noble standing cupboard, which in the hands of the French or Dutch would have developed fine proportions, is marred by a want of symmetry in its component parts. Some good specimens of ancient Flemish furniture were to be seen before the great war at the Musée d'Art Industriel Ancien in Brussels, and the Musée Plantin, Antwerp, where, in the dwelling portion, the presses, cupboards, and chests used by the Plantin family during the sixteenth and seventeenth centuries remained in their original surroundings.

Towards the end of the sixteenth and during the following century the Flemings were very partial to split-pendants and balusters applied to the stiles of their furniture. Ornaments of applied strap, perforated in fretwork, were also fastened on the uprights, giving an appearance of richness, which is very pleasing. The latter custom does not appear to have become fashionable in England, where such ornament was almost invariably carved from the solid. The doors of oak cabinets and cupboards were also quartered into geometrical panels, but the proportions and effect were distinctly different from similar methods of framing used by French or English craftsmen. Marquetry, as employed by the Flemings, was often overdone and in doubtful taste, the execution being mostly inferior to embellishments of the same nature executed by either French or Germans.

The Flemish Baroque, or decadence of the Renaissance style, is perhaps as ugly and unmeaning as any declension in Europe. Effects were perpetrated which occasionally give one the impression of explosions in wood or unexpected accidents happening to the stage scenery. These, however, are for the most part to be found in churches, domestic furniture partaking more heavily in their appropriations of French and German characteristics, and exhibiting a combination of the baser methods of both nations.

PLATE VI.

RENAISSANCE FRENCH COFFER.

Victoria and Albert Museum.

CHAPTER V.

TYROLESE FURNITURE.

IN Tyrolese carving a peculiarity exists which can hardly fail to be noticed, even by novices. The decorative designs are made by outlined incisions, leaving the upper surface of the sculpture perfectly flat, and not moulded in any way. In fact, the objects represented may almost be termed silhouettes. Markings on scrolls, animals, mythical creatures and the like, are all indicated by slight incisions, modelled surfaces being avoided. The lower planes in the sculpture—the " field," if an heraldic term may be employed—are frequently coloured with vermilion, red ochre, and black, accentuating the flat, outlined objects, which are represented on the higher surfaces. The locks, lock-plates, and iron fittings generally, are very elaborate and decorative in character, displaying a profusion of wrought foliation and scroll-work, generally backed with scarlet cloth, after the German manner, and of which traces may sometimes be found on existing specimens.

The staple material of which Tyrolese furniture is constructed is fir; no doubt chiefly owing to the indigenous nature of that wood, but perhaps also in a small measure due to the singular immunity which it possesses from the attacks of both moth and worm.* It is probably these latter qualities which have been instrumental in saving so many specimens of early Tyrolese work from the wreck of old estates which for a hundred years and more devastated the district. From what is left it may be safely assumed that the quantity of fine productions in the shape of furniture must have been immense, the thick forests which cover nearly half the country contributing easily to the manufacture of furniture by the craftsman. Another singularity in Tyrolese decoration is the survival of Gothic characteristics in pieces made in times when such features had been fairly abandoned by the rest of Europe. The chest belonging to Sir Coleridge Grove, which figures in the illustration on Plate LXVII., is an example of how pieces were produced in the seventeenth century bearing very elegant Gothic tracery, accompanied by debased arches and the undisputed dates of their construction. There is not a few of these anomalies about, and their apparent contradictions are not unfrequently puzzling to the amateur. Occasionally other enigmas arise in connection with specimens connected with this group. For purposes of cross reference the typical Tyrolese coffer, bearing an English inscription, now in the Victoria and Albert Museum, may be briefly noted here, though it is more fully debated on in the chapter entitled " English or Foreign ? ".

Some of the early fruit of Tyrolese craftsmen is intensely original and artistic

---

* Cedar and walnut were also occasionally used, the latter wood being mainly employed in the shape of inlay.

in its imagining, composite pieces answering the several purposes of cupboard and settle, chest and dresser, being contrived in a way which could hardly have been excelled in any other country in Europe. Towards Bavaria the characteristic flat-surfaced carving began to be mingled with a more modulated contour, and especially in the neighbourhood of Munich the splendidly elaborate scroll and foliated work in high relief, so distinctive of the Teutonic sculptors, asserted itself. A combination of these two methods of decoration on one article often presents a very agreeable sense of relief.

The Tyrol, in common with many other parts, may no longer be considered the happy hunting-ground of the collector, though examples of the National Art may still be purchased there, but at prices of an altitude out of all proportion with those of a decade or so ago. Indeed, some of the amounts at which these relics were acquired by museums and pioneer collectors would hardly purchase a good deal table with its ordinary accompaniments. But that is forty years or so ago, and nowadays the Tyrol is scoured as much as many other hunting-grounds in Europe.

The ingenuity of the old Tyrolese craftsman in planning fixed furniture such as combined settles and dressers, or seats and cupboards, has been somewhat revived by so-called art furniture designers in our own country within recent years, but much has to be accomplished before ancient specimens can be successfully competed with. The simple needs of the living-room have to be more seriously studied than a mere striving for effect. Once this desideratum is recognised, true picturesqueness may follow as a natural result.

CHAPTER VI.

SOME FRESH FIGURED EXAMPLES.

HAVE dealt elsewhere with the group of knightly examples, which, for purposes of classification, I have dubbed with the imaginative title of "Tilting Coffers." * The description of this very rare type included specimens at Harty, Kent; Southwold, Suffolk; York Minster; Ypres, Belgium; and the Victoria and Albert and Cluny Museums. Since the publication of the works dealing with this subject, one or two other prototypes of a similar kind have come to light, which are fully as interesting as any hitherto described. The most important of the fresh examples is a coffer-front now at New College, Oxford, bearing a somewhat confused but remarkable carving, evidently intended for the battle of Courtrai, which occurred between the Flemings and the French in the year 1302. The banners of the various Flemish guilds are depicted, as well as various incidents in the combat, and though somewhat clumsy in execution, this piece is replete in historical interest of a definite kind. The arms of Pierre Coninc, one of the Flemish leaders, are shown on one of the banners, and, it is said, are to be found on no other records except on a seal in the archives of Bruges. This coffer-front was debated upon at some length at the Society of Antiquaries on 19th March, 1914, when an exceedingly able and descriptive paper was read by Mr. C. ffoulkes, Keeper of the Tower Armoury, who made out a very good case for a curious weapon with which the men gathered under the Flemish banners are depicted as being armed, and which he identified with the "Godendag," or "plançon à picot," a species of club topped with a spike, which is mentioned by the chronicler Guiart as being in use about this date. As regards the general mode of decoration, a very extraordinary survival of an earlier epoch is discernible in the crowding of the figures in a sort of processionary movement into longitudinal compartments placed one above the other on the same panel. The Franks casket, of Anglo-Saxon workmanship, in the British Museum, is treated in a similar manner, and there are many parallelisms between the methodical treatments of these widely dissociated pieces.

Nothing is actually known about the history of this coffer-front except that it formed an item among some goods taken in lieu of rent of an Oxfordshire farm some years ago. But circumstantial history in such absorbing relics is seldom silent, and some attempt has been made to connect this coffer-front with the great poet Chaucer. The "father of English literature," as he is termed, married a Flemish lady, and owned a demesne in the vicinity of the farm from whence the coffer-front

---

* *Ancient Coffers and Cupboards* (Methuen, 1902); *Old Oak Furniture* (Methuen).

came, and it is also known that Chaucer conducted secret-service work in Flanders
in the years 1376-7.   But proof of any sort of the association is wanting.   The
costume and equipment of the figures more nearly approximate to the date of the
battle of Courtrai than to Chaucer's sixty years or so, ending with 1400; but while
there is no reason that Chaucer should not have possessed a piece of furniture some
seventy or more years old, it is hardly feasible to suppose that so heavy and militant
a piece would have taken the form of a dower chest to the poet's wife.   The conjecture
raised is certainly interesting, but it is purely presumptive, and lacks any real
supporting evidence.   That the subjects depicted were intended for incidents
connected with the battle of Courtrai, where the obstinate valour of the Flemish
burghers repulsed the fiery charges of the chivalry of France, there can be hardly
any doubt, but beyond this one can scarcely venture.   It is to be hoped that discussion
on this relic may help to bring into prominence other pieces of a like nature.

The second specimen in this class which appears to have escaped any serious
notice is a carved and coloured wooden panel which hangs on the north wall of
St. George's Church, Norwich.   The subject represented in the sculpture is the
patron saint's encounter with the dragon, and though later in date than the
better known specimens at York, Ypres, and South Kensington, has some of the
features of the coffers bearing the same theme.   This panel evidently formed part
of the muniment coffer of the very church in which it now remains.   At present it
is in a very bad position for examination.

A coffer-front of the fifteenth century, exhibiting extraordinary characteristics, is
possessed by Colonel Walter Horsley, of Cranbrook, Kent, which may well be
included among the figured examples.   The tracery which adorns this interesting
fragment is unmistakably English, but apparently the craftsman who executed the
carving was in such a hurry to commence his task that he quite neglected to set out
the design beforehand.   The piece belongs to a time and type of which we have none
too many examples remaining, but what specially enhances its interest is the fact that
above the traceried arches appears the representation of a female head, gardant, and
bearing the enormous double-horned head-dress so typical of the period.   The lady's
head (which is uncomplimentary to the sex) is accompanied by coarse chimeras, while
on the sinister upright is carved an unequivocal devil of hideous aspect.   The opposite
upright is decorated with a shield bearing a saltier engrailed, on the dexter side a
martlet.   On that end of the panel nearest the shield appears a demon's head,
the tracery of the windows being "broken," or interrupted, to admit the insertion
of the solitary black letter **t**.   The whole design is in a weird and fantastic vein,
the figures being of a morbid nature reminiscent of the old "Dooms."   Read the riddle
who can of this cryptic and singular relic.   Its history is unknown, beyond the
certainty that it has been in its present abode for at least forty years.

Very different as regards quality are some of the pieces in the collection of wood
carvings formed by the Rev. Philip Nelson, of Calderstones, Liverpool.   These are
partly heraldic in character, and indicate such a high state of art that it is a matter
for regret so little remains.   In particular, one magnificent fragment of panelling

which was discovered during some repairs at Docker Hall, Lancashire, is the finest of its kind, the knightly figures, armed in harness of the fifteenth century, being designed with exceptional skill and fidelity. We frequently find circumstantial attributions tacked on to roughly executed pieces—such as the armoire at South Kensington, or the Courtrai panel—based, perhaps, on little more than their discovery near some ancient manor, while here is a remnant of the highest class obviously made for a personage of great distinction about which no conjecture seems to have been hazarded.

The breaking up of a piece of antique furniture almost always destroys much evidence as to its origin. The carving of human figures, whether French, English, or otherwise, may possess points of similarity, but the reaving of a panel from its framing can have no other effect than to get rid of any proof which its attendant mouldings might afford, especially in the case of objects dating from the fifteenth and early sixteenth centuries. It may be accepted as a truism that the English designer or craftsman invariably abstained from the intersection of mouldings on the corners of framed panels which characterises so much of the continental work. Elimination of contributory evidence of the mouldings has, I feel sure, been responsible for many errors of judgment in descriptions attached to objects deposited in our museums. How important the foregoing thesis is may be at once grasped when the mouldings are not attached to the framing, but carved on the surface of the panel, and, consequently, have not been destroyed when the breaking-up process occurred. Even in the latter instance such manifestations are not always fully weighed. Two little credence panels which have recently been acquired for the Victoria and Albert Museum are a case in point. These pieces, which date from the junction of the fifteenth and sixteenth centuries, have, superficially, a Flemish twist about their sculpture, though perhaps not enough to give absolute denial to the description which is attached to them: "English, about 1500. W. 5-6, 1911." If, however, the intersection of the mouldings on these panels had been properly regarded, I venture to think that this decision would have been a different one. The point is one well known in the architectural profession, but does not appear to have been sufficiently considered by many critics of antique oak. Here, again, the same difficulty may present itself as to the precise meaning of the word "foreign," but I may say that I know of no instance in which pieces of oak furniture exhibiting these intersecting members can, on close examination, be rightly referred to as of English origin, either as regards design or execution.

CHAPTER VII.

Secret Receptacles and Treasure Chests.

 FAIR amount of ancient church coffers still exist which retain their original hiding-places in various forms, sometimes in the shape of a false bottom to the body of the coffer itself, but more often fitted beneath the little tray which is almost invariably attached to one of its ends. An example of the first type remains in the parvise of the parish church at Newport, Essex—an exceedingly rare and beautiful specimen of ancient English furniture, which is more fully described in another of my works; while instances of the secret tray-bottom may be found in coffers existing in the churches of Long Stanton St. Michael, Cambs.; Stoke d'Abernon, Surrey; and Rogate and Bosham, Sussex. That the hiding-places in these ancient coffers were sometimes hastily emptied, there is every reason to believe, and we have evidence of this in at least one case in Southern England. The coffer at Bosham, just mentioned, is a plain, heavy production, unornamented except for dwarf pilasters at the base of its huge uprights, and some chamfering on the lid flanges and inner tray lid. A few years ago a thorough examination of this coffer was instituted by the incumbent, with the result that a silver Waterford halfpenny, dating from the reign of Edward I., was discovered in the secret well beneath the tray. Though the device must have been fairly well known to the craftsmen of the thirteenth century, it was sufficiently ingenious and mute to have safeguarded its secret during several dynasties.

But, nevertheless, repetition must have ventilated this secret more or less, for we find that changes occurred in the fashion and devising of concealed receptacles, which proves that in some contemporary cases discovery must have been suspected or else taken place. All the coffers just mentioned belong to the thirteenth century; after that the tray-well was discarded, only to reappear in a few examples made in Elizabethan times.* It is evident that some novel device or custom appealed to the patron or cofferer, and the old contrivance not only became obsolete, but entirely disused and forgotten. A few specimens of later improvisation may be mentioned.

In the early part of 1913 a Tudor oak buffet was sold at Messrs. Christie, Manson & Woods', which contained two secret receptacles enclosed by sliding panels in the front. This buffet was a very elaborate specimen of workmanship, and fetched the large sum of £840 under the hammer, despite certain indications that seemed to hint attentions at the hand of the restorer.

A seventeenth-century French armoire known to the writer possesses a very artful hiding-place for money *in the foot of each of its uprights*—a very unusual position for such receptacles.

It is not till we reach the borders of the seventeenth century that court cupboards

---

* The late Mr. Ernest Crofts, R.A., possessed several family pieces of oak dating from the commencement of the seventeenth century which retained hiding-places of this description.

PLATE VII.

WALNUT-WOOD CABINET.   SECOND HALF OF SIXTEENTH CENTURY.   FRENCH (LYONS).
Victoria and Albert Museum.

attain the little secret ledge or shelf over their top cupboards which may be found in so many English examples. To those who know not this simple peculiarity, it may be briefly explained that it generally exists in recessed pieces of the court cupboard class, immediately between the cornice moulding and the niche underneath, and may be easily found by opening one of the small upper doors in the recess and placing the hand upwards in the crevice formed by the canopy. A somewhat well-known and obvious place of concealment, even at the time when such pieces were in fashion, it is little more than a hidden shelf, and could hardly have been used except for temporary purposes of secretion; yet it nowadays often escapes notice, and since the old style of court cupboard has ceased to be made, except by fakers and imitators, this humble hiding-place often remains undiscovered for an indefinite time, just as the secret wells in the coffers of the thirteenth century rested *perdu* once the fashion of their making was over.

But such "secrets," as they were sometimes termed, could hardly have been intended to receive treasure of any bulk, or objects which for ordinary safety would frankly be locked up in the strong box of the time. The iron-bound treasure-chests such as we usually associate with the Great Armada or the safe-keeping of early muniments, are merely cumbrous, unornamental affairs, and proclaim boldly without disguise that they defy any attempt at unlawful opening. A great many of the latter specimens, both wood and iron, possess false or dummy lock-plates, intended to deceive the would-be thief, though this custom was so well known at the time of their construction that it is hard to believe that many intellects could have been duped by so shallow a pretence.

Wonderful stories are told of these so-called Armada relics, many of them of quite a circumstantial nature, and by far the greater part absolutely without foundation. The screen and gallery in Middle Temple Hall, a typical piece of English carving dating from 1575, has similarly been asserted to have come from one of the captured Spanish galleons, and this absurd and preposterous fallacy is still believed and spread by many ignorant people. Most of the iron-sheathed strong boxes to be found in our municipal museums have legends of this description attaching to them. Such fables are as numerous as the stories about Cromwell, and certainly on the whole as baseless.

Amongst the wonderful collection of objects connected with the City of London, gathered together in the Guildhall Museum, are four typical specimens of the iron strong-box of the sixteenth and seventeenth centuries, about which a certain amount of record is known. The first three are the ancient muniment-coffers of the Ship-wrights', the Feltmakers', and the Plumbers' Companies; the fourth formerly filling the same purpose for the Church of St. Vedast, in Foster Lane, a building which was only partially demolished by the Great Fire of 1666. All these coffers have complicated locks inside their lids, provided with from ten to thirteen bolts, as well as hasps and padlocks on their exteriors. The coffer which formerly belonged to the Worshipful Company of Shipwrights is furthermore fitted on one side with an inner box, a sort of survival of the Gothic tray, affixed, however, to the bottom and not to the upper part, as in earlier examples. All these three municipal guild-chests were presented to the Museum by their respective companies.

Examples of treasure-chests of wood bound or sheathed in iron are numerous, and may be seen at Salisbury and Wells Cathedrals; the West Gate, Winchester; the Town Hall, Fordwich, Kent; the Rolls Museum in Chancery Lane, and a hundred other places. The various dates of their construction are often obscure and difficult to detect, as some trifling peculiarity in construction of fitting is frequently the only detail which affords any light upon the subject. We have, however, some evidence of the approximate genesis of the Winchester example, as it is known to have been made to replace an older one which was broken into by thieves in 1590, when the city seals and plate and " four score pounds " were carried off. The ringed handles for transport at each end of the coffer are noticeable. See Plate XLII.

We have an interesting record of the sums disbursed for the construction of the iron-bound coffer which exists in Ashburton Church, Devonshire. In the year 1482-3, " John Soper, for sawing — feet of timber," was paid two shillings and four-pence, while " John Clyff, for making one chest," received the sum of 6d. The said box was apparently not considered strong enough, for six years later a " Mr. Half-hyde " received 13s. 10¼d. " for iron and making the same for binding the great chest," while a locksmith was remunerated with the sum of 5s. 9d. for making the locks and keys. These several items, which appear to be singularly disproportionate, are recorded in the churchwardens' accounts, which have luckily been preserved.

Instances of the discovery of treasure-chests containing their original contents intact are exceedingly rare in our own country, but they still occur occasionally, and always in totally unexpected places. As an example of how treasure may be quite lost sight of when it remains disused, the strange discoveries in Rochester may be quoted. The old treasury attached to the cathedral lately underwent a very neces-sary process of restoration, as the room had been practically disused for a long period. According to a writer in *The Times* of May 4th, 1914, " few people have been aware of the existence of the old room, part of the original Norman structure, or of the chief of the treasures which it contains. Only at intervals of years, so far as is known, have human feet trod the winding staircase which leads to the apartment. No one really seems to have cared what was contained in the great sixteenth-century chest, which must have been built inside the room, for there is not, and seemingly has never been, a door large enough to admit of its being carried through in its entirety.* If there ever was a list of the cathedral plate it has long been lost and forgotten, and some of the almost priceless pieces of silver which have been in use in the cathedral were commonly supposed to be of brass. The old staircase had become almost unclimbable, and the room itself was choked with the accumulated dust of, literally, centuries."

---

* The custom of building large coffers inside the treasuries and parvises of ecclesiastical buildings was a common one, the main reason probably being that in the event of failure on the part of thieves to break open such receptacles, it would be impossible to transport them bodily away through openings too small to allow them to pass. The painted coffer in Newport Church, Essex, is an example.—AUTHOR.

The result of this much-desired spring cleaning was the bringing to light a quantity of long-forgotten plate of the most valuable description, chief among which were two beautiful dishes (*ciboria*) of the date 1530-1533. They are 5 inches high and 9 inches wide, and have between them one cover. It is conjectured that there was originally but one, which was transferable to either of the vessels. These relics, the discovery of which provided quite a sensation, are now exhibited in the renovated treasury among other archæological valuables appertaining to the cathedral.

Accounts of discoveries of a somewhat similar nature to the last occasionally reach us from the Continent, and one or two startling examples are given here.

In 1907, while excavating in the streets of Madrid, some labourers unearthed an old chest of walnut wood, which, on being opened, was found to contain 300 doubloons, valued at about £1,400 of our money at the time.

In 1912 a discovery of exceptional importance was made in the village of Malaia Pereshtchepina, in the Province of Poltava, in south-west Russia. Some farm labourers, while digging in a field, uncovered a decayed coffer, which was found to contain a quantity of dishes, utensils, and ornaments of gold and silver, as well as some 450 gold and 50 silver coins, some of the latter dating back as far as the fourth century A.D. Owing to the fact that the coins and plates were alike considerably discoloured, the labourers, possibly because they could not believe in the existence of so great amount of treasure, persisted in regarding the ornaments and utensils as being of lead and brass, and divided their spoil between them, retaining it in their cottages. At length the news of this discovery got about, and on examination being made, the contents of the chest was found to include the following objects:—a large silver dish of very ancient origin, damascened in gold, and bearing a Latin inscription showing it to be in the possession of a bishop living in the eleventh century; a similar dish embossed with the image of a Persian monarch living in the fourth century; eleven solid gold cups of Persian make, and a quantity of bracelets and ornaments, as well as several silver cups of Byzantine workmanship. The collection was exhibited in its entirety at the State Bank, and it was estimated that the aggregate value amounted to the astonishing sum of £100,000. An announcement was made that the owner of the land on which the treasure was found and the labourers who made the actual discovery would divide the value of the treasure between them—an exceedingly unwise proceeding, but probably more or less very problematical of accomplishment.

Such finds of equipped treasure-chests may be excessively rare, but we are, nevertheless, occasionally startled in our own country by the bringing to light from some long-disused and forgotten receptacle of objects hardly less precious. As an addition to our national relics, a discovery made at Colchester in 1907 may be classed among the most interesting made in recent years. The church of St. Giles, memorable as being the burial-place of the two Royalist supporters, Sir Charles Lucas and Sir George Lisle, who were shot by order of General Fairfax after the siege of Colchester, was during the year mentioned undergoing a thorough restoration. An old oak chest in the vestry, which seems to have remained in a neglected condition, was opened and emptied, with the result that there was found a purple cloth in excellent preservation bearing the insignia of the Lucas family and the date 1617. Whether this once formed the pall of the family mentioned, or whether its purpose had been the draping of the altar in the Lucas Chapel on the south side of the church, is doubtful; but it seems likely that the relic had been secreted under the mass of documents with which the chest was filled in order to escape unwelcome notice and possible destruction. Putting a different construction on the term "treasure" than that employed in the cases previously mentioned, this discovery would be somewhat hard to beat.

In days when property was insecure, and the only recognised bankers were the goldsmiths, many very ingenious devices were adopted in articles of domestic use. These were perpetuated through the decadent period of oak, the conservative instincts of ownership often resulting in a continuity which has descended to the present day. The annexed instances (latter-day discoveries culled at random) were perhaps made from no very early depositories, but the hiding-places kept their secrets indifferently well, though they must have possessed scores, and most likely hundreds, of duplicates.

"A story which will set antique dealers examining all their stock for secret drawers comes from Cardiff. Mr. Muller, an antique dealer of that city, bought a bureau at a sale last November for £3. While Mrs. Muller was examining the bureau on Wednesday, she accidentally touched a secret button, which opened a hidden drawer, and in that drawer she found securities of the value of £1,000, in the name of David Morris Lewis. A daughter of this Mr. Lewis has been traced by the police, and it was explained that when Mr. Lewis died, six years ago, his family were surprised to find how little property he had left."—*Daily Express*, 18th April, 1913.

At Birmingham, in 1908, the breaking up of an old family chest for firewood led to the discovery of a false bottom containing one hundred perfect spade guineas, worth some 25s. each.

A rummage sale was held on the rectory lawn at Beardmore, Hants., in 1910, when an old writing-desk changed hands for the sum of eighteenpence. Owing to rough handling a secret drawer subsequently fell out, and with it thirty gold coins—guineas and half-guineas of the reign of George III.

Announcements such as these crop up almost every month, and, alas! their publication not infrequently results in much furniture smashing by ignorant persons in their desire to acquire a proportion of unearned increment.

There are also many instances of coffers, chests, and cupboards which, having no secret hiding-places, yet possess some ingenious contrivance for concealing the locks or key-holes which secure their contents. A very customary and favourite expedient adopted by the Dutch and Flemish craftsmen may be specially described. In cabinets and cupboards possessing folding doors, the façades are often enriched with moulded pilasters of a classic character, the centre one of which is attached close to the edge of the overlapping door. The upper portion of the shaft of this column was made to slide horizontally for an inch or so, thus bringing the keyhole into view. A simple contrivance, and plentiful enough at one time, it may be that the craftsman would not allow the lock to interfere with his original design, for the amount of secrecy involved could obviously have been but moderate, and the device must have been constantly liable to discovery owing to the recurrence of surface polishing, which was so religiously kept up in the Low Countries. The ornate Dutch cabinet illustrated on Plate LVI. is fitted with this mechanism.

An English device of somewhat similar character, but of greater scarcity, is fully described in the chapter on "Furniture bearing Dates."

A fairly recent sensation in the way of discoveries is that of the register of the Black Prince, which was unearthed from an old iron box in the keeping of a firm of solicitors of very old standing. The following interesting account of it appeared in the *Daily Mail*, May, 1914.

The box "remained till 1878 in a vault of the firm in Bloomsbury. Then it was transferred to a Holborn street, where, after crossing the road, it remained till 1913.

"A responsible clerk who entered the service of the firm in 1863 was told by his predecessor, when he first took over his duties, that there was a 'diary' of the Black Prince in a large oak chest, and the head of the firm occasionally used to refer to it by this name; but nothing was ever done in the way of examining the volume.

"It was only last year, when the premises were finally transferred to the Inns of Court district, that the new head of the firm, being told of the existence of the 'diary,' determined to have the large oak chest (some 6 feet by 3 feet) and various other receptacles for documents, including two rusty sheet-iron boxes, overhauled.

"A number of interesting documents, including a fourteenth-century law book and a chancellery roll of Fountains Abbey, were found in the oak chest. In one of the two partitions of the old sheet-iron box, so rusty that the bottom was almost falling out, was lying the register of the Black Prince covered by a bundle of deeds. This was in the last days of April of last year.

"The volume was soon afterwards submitted to one of the foremost experts in the country, who at once recognised its authenticity. With the owners' permission he submitted it to Sir Henry Maxwell-Lyte, Deputy-Keeper of the Record Office, who declared it to be the missing volume of a series of three registers of 1350 to 1365, the other two of which are in the possession of the Record Office, the one relating to Chester properties, the other to Cornish properties of the Prince.

"The volume then returned to the possession of its owner. . . . Whether the volume will pass into the hands of a private collector or of the State the future will show."

Among the items included in the volume the following are of special interest to students of the history of furniture:—

"'Robert Joyner' received 60 shillings for three chairs, and for a leather-bound coffer 13 shillings and four pence."

Of all discoveries in the shape of historical literature the last-mentioned is surely one of the most astonishing made within recent years.

D

CHAPTER VIII.

FURNITURE BEARING DATES.

IT would be difficult to classify and impossible to enumerate even approximately a tithe of the manifold examples of dated furniture remaining in this country. Private collections and noble and manorial residences abound in them, sales forced by death or other contingencies occasionally bringing to light treasures well-nigh as hidden as the Gothic crypts beneath our London soil. References, to be of any use to the multitude, can only be made to certain typical and accessible specimens, which may be studied freely, and their diverse dates compared with the structure and decoration of the pieces which exhibit them.

It must be borne in mind that the terms "early" and "late" are comparative, and what would be an early *dated* chest would probably belong to no earlier age than that of Philip and Mary or Elizabeth. Of thirteenth-century coffers we possess a plenitude, but I am not aware that any of them bears the veritable year of construction upon it. On the other hand, the majority of dates actually appearing on furniture belong to the seventeenth century, any previous to the last quarter of the sixteenth being of the greatest rarity.

One of the earliest dated examples of furniture in our own country is the coffer in Shanklin Church, Isle of Wight. This beautiful instance of Early Renaissance art is carved on its front with the letters "T. S.," formed out of the elaborate scroll-work so typical of the reigns of Henry VII. and Henry VIII. Running round these letters is a band, bearing the inscription:—

"DOMINUS THOMAS SILKSTED PRIOR. ANNO DNI 1519."

Underneath the lock appear the arms of the See of Winchester, of which Thomas Silksted was prior from 1498 till his death in 1524. The Lady Chapel at Winchester Cathedral (the latest portion of that edifice) was completed by him after having been commenced by Prior Hunton, his predecessor. It is seldom, indeed, that the origin of a movable piece of furniture is so clearly indicated by its carved decoration as in the case of this fine coffer.

Various conjectures have been made as to the reasons why so many Italian secretaires and nests of drawers should have been placed on obviously English stands. I think the riddle is not very difficult to solve. These products of Italy were in their own country mostly placed on side-tables, which, for some reason, may not have accorded with English taste or convenience, the result being that it is not uncommon in our land to find superstructures of distinctly Italian make associated with contemporary English stands. In our illustration (Plate XLIV.) the secretaire, which is made of camphor or cypress wood, is dated in two places 1594, while the under-stand is decorated with typical Elizabethan strap-work, carved in English oak. A curious feature may be noticed in the inscription, running round three sides of the front panel, which indicates that the craftsman who produced this piece must have been somewhat casual in the setting out of his lettering. The inscription reads thus :—

113533

DEVSINNOMINETVOSALVVEMEFACEINVIRTVTETVAIVDICAME

At first sight, the legend appears to consist of a chaotic collection of letters, the order of which becomes apparent upon careful study. It will be noticed that the sign of abbreviation over the V should have been over the ME, the T of the ET being omitted, and that the carver miscalculated his distance to such an extent that he actually found it necessary to enclose an I and an A within two other letters at the end of the inscription in an exceedingly quaint way. The ME which the inscription finished with has been partly cut away at some time or another, apparently to make the falling lid fit. Contrast between Italian and English workmanship is very noticeable in this international product, the chip-carving of the Southerns being essentially lighter and more classic than the sculpture on the beautiful Elizabethan oak section.

A very beautiful English court cupboard of the time of James I., which has recently been acquired by the authorities of the Victoria and Albert Museum (W. 32), is of oak, carved and inlaid, bearing on its centre panel, underneath the canopy, the initials H M, while the small doors to right and left of this panel are inlaid with the date "ANNO—1610." No locks are visible on the upper tier, but on each side of the centre panel, separating it from the doors, is a heavily-moulded pilaster, the upper part of which is capable of being raised, when the keyhole is at once disclosed to view. This contrivance is a rare variation of the Dutch peculiarity mentioned in the chapter on "Secret Receptacles." The upper doors of this valuable and interesting cupboard are inlaid with geometrical patterns, and the frieze is carved with elaborate "jewel moulding," the lower doors being plainly panelled. Though missing its "cock's-head" hinges on the under story, this exhibit is in an exceptionally fine state of preservation, and is one of the best and most typical of its kind.

At the time of writing, a very good Jacobean court cupboard is at the "Cheshire Cheese" in Fleet Street. This piece, which is of plain and Puritanical aspect, exhibits the inscription—

T
G D
1626

which seems somewhat to antedate its accepted type.

Tables of the Elizabethan and Jacobean periods were frequently carved with the dates of their construction, the figures being usually distributed on two of the uprights and separated by the stretchers. A great number of these tables remain all over England, located mainly in churches, where they have been used for purposes of Holy Communion since Reformation times, but also to be found occasionally in manor halls and farmhouses of the better class. The fine jewel-moulded specimen in Dinton Church, Bucks., dated 1606, described in my work on *Old Oak Furniture*, is a specific instance of this type.* Though such dates, if present, were almost invariably carved on the uprights of these tables and not on the stretchers, they were not always distributed on different uprights, as in the Dinton example, but were sometimes incised on one alone, with, occasionally, the maker's mark or initials branded beside them.

A genuine trencher-table belonging to the Royal School of Needlework was among the objects on loan at the Exhibition of Ancient Furniture opened in 1914 at the Geffrye Almshouses in Kingsland Road. This table was probably originally intended for an altar or side-table, as the front rail alone was carved. The legs were rather heavy in character, and on one of them appeared the genuine date, 1648, together with the maker's mark, "T ᙠ."

Another piece of very great interest included in the same exhibition was a small oak desk, carved on all four sides with geometrical whorles, and on the lid with the arms of Oliver Cromwell, accompanied by the date 1659. The carving was small and somewhat Dutch in character, and had the appearance of being contemporary; the interior had been fitted with drawers, only one of which remained, bearing the inlaid inscription, "I S 1779." According to tradition, this desk was given by the Protector to Bernard Gomme, the engineer of Tilbury Forts, in the seventeenth century, its modern possessor being the late Sir Laurence Gomme.

A curious little Flemish coffer in the Victoria and Albert Museum (410—1911), shaped something in the form of a housemaid's box, is dated in iron figures 1556, accompanied by the initials "D. P. D." The wood is also clasped with ornamental bands of iron, and the lid is formed out of a very massive linen-panel, which, from its thickness, might have been removed from some church door. The type is an unusual one.

Many boxes in English country churches exhibit carved inscriptions, accompanied by dates, though these are mostly pieces somewhat late in character.

At Combs, Suffolk, is an oak-panelled chest inscribed with the comparatively early date 1599, while in the adjoining county of Norfolk a chest dated 1632 exists in the parish church of Great Snoring.

A very curious and interesting chest, dating from the first half of the seventeenth century, is that remaining in the parish church of Norton St. Philip, Somerset. This relic bears on its front the somewhat involved inscription :—

THOMAᴢ	IOHN . ME
16 ᴢTENT	REFELD 34
CHURCH	WARDENS.

---

* The Dinton table has been painted an abominable buff colour, through which the traces of inlay can be distinctly seen.

Local taste (!) has of recent years mounted this chest upon legs, by which its appearance is by no means improved.

In the parish church of Blundeston, Suffolk (famed as the Blunderstone of *David Copperfield*), is an oak chest of a latish type, scored with a crude pattern on its stiles and panels. This piece, compared with the beautiful poppy-heads which ornament the bench ends in the same church, is indeed a poor specimen, but a certain amount of interest attaches to it inasmuch that *inside* the lid appears the date 1640, accompanied by the initials of two people, most probably those of the churchwardens in office at the genesis of its use. This is a striking instance of the difficulty of assigning even fairly definite dates to some pieces of antique oak, as before seeing the inscription (an undoubtedly genuine one) nineteen authorities out of twenty would mentally "place" the piece as being considerably later in the seventeenth century.

What is most probably one of the largest boxes in England must be included in the present section. It exists in the parish church of Scarcliffe, near Mansfield, Derbyshire, and is an enormous production, measuring some ten feet in length, the lid bearing the incised inscription, " F. H. 1671." * Derbyshire is singularly rich in the possession of chests and coffers, even when those at Haddon are not considered. A specimen at Chelmorton in this county is carved with the somewhat pompous inscription :—

RALPH BUXTON OF FLAGG GAVE THIS 1630.

Among iron-bound church coffers exhibiting dates one very remarkable London example may be specially mentioned, which, though easily accessible, is not as well known or studied as it should be. This relic is the muniment coffer of the church of St. Giles-in-the-Fields, and though passed every day by connoisseurs and lovers of such rarities, remains almost unknown and unobserved. The coffer, which stands upon curious clawed feet, is bound with bands of iron, alternatively plain or perforated with strapwork decoration in the Carolean style. The date 1630, with the initials of the contemporary trustees, as well as the Royal Supporters and various coats of arms, appear on the front and lid of this coffer, the ornamentation being ingeniously carried out in wrought iron. St. Giles's Church was erected between the years 1720 and 1734, replacing an older structure of red brick, which was consecrated by Laud in 1623, and the coffer just mentioned is evidently a survival from the earlier building. It is singular that Metropolitan histories, none of which forget to mention such circumstances as the association of the church with the Tyburn Tree journey or the tomb of Richard Penderel in its churchyard, should so persistently ignore the existence of this valuable and interesting relic, while often remarking upon the paucity of interest within St. Giles's walls.

Of other dated specimens appertaining to church furniture, the poor-box in Dovercourt Church, Essex, should be noted. A ponderous lump of oak, strongly

---

* The largest is a thirteenth-century coffer at Westminster Abbey, which measures close upon thirteen feet long.

bound with plain straps of iron, this relic exhibits the date 1589, the year following the dispersion of the Spanish Armada, when generosity towards the Protestant poor was harshly modified by the fines and penalties inflicted upon recusants and Papists.

Among alms-boxes of subsequent dates to the above, the following may be noted: Bramford, Suffolk, 1591; Aylestone, Leicester, 1613; Clapham, Bedford, 1627; Sedbergh, Yorks., 1633; Manton, Rutland, 1637; Bletchley, Bucks., 1637; Lostwithiel, Cornwall, 1645; while the number of others remaining bearing various dates during the seventeenth century indicates that the custom of recording the years in which these receptacles of benevolence were made was a very general one.

A little oak cupboard in the historical gate-house at Rye House is worthy of mention, as it is dated 1659, and yet possesses the inlay of mother-o'-pearl and bone which is usually associated with the elaborate Dutch features which are seen on English-made pieces after the Restoration. The same advanced method of decoration may be noticed on an even earlier piece, dated 1653, in the Victoria and Albert Museum.

Among the many curious confirmations of the tulipomania which spread from Holland to England in the seventeenth century, an interesting example may be cited in a portion of a chest-front in the little museum at Aylesbury. Towards the end of the seventeenth century the mania was probably at its height, and the long-forgotten owner of this piece, who was evidently something of an enthusiast, has recorded his predilection by adorning the box with conventional forms of tulips, accompanied by the legend, "16 E H 92."

Chairs do not appear to have been so commonly inscribed with the dates of their construction as coffers and chests, though a goodly number remain which have initials or other evidences of ownership attached to them, which in some cases may assist to determine the approximate date at which they were made.

In the north transept of Oundle Church, Northants., is a curiosity in the shape of a chair of rude semi-Gothic form, bearing the inscription:—

SUMPTV◇AP ℳMATO I ℳA ℳN LONDINENSIVM◇A.D.◇1576.

This relic is so weird and unusual that to place any reliance on its style as appertaining to the period in which it was dated would be misleading. It should be compared with the more accepted example, dated 1560, which stands in the chancel of Epworth Parish Church, Lincolnshire.

The custom of attaching the year of their manufacture to articles of furniture was not confined solely to the woodwork of such pieces. Chairs with stuffed backs and seats were sometimes provided with such dates executed in needlework. A low-backed chair of this type in the Victoria and Albert Museum is embroidered with a floral pattern in coloured wools after the manner of a carpet, the date 1649 appearing on its back. It is, of course, quite possible that the embroidery, which is worked on a canvas covering stretched over the seat and back of the chair, may have been carried out a few years after the framework, but the twisted rails of the latter seem to indicate a confirmation of the accompanying date, as spiral members did not come really into vogue until about the middle of the century, though they may have been made in inconsiderable numbers at a slightly earlier date.

During the Elizabethan and Jacobean eras, bedsteads were probably more frequently carved with the dates of their origin than any other article of furniture. The great increase in the area of glass for lighting purposes, which was an architectural feature of the former epoch, resulted in discomfort in the shape of draughts, rendering it necessary to construct the bedsteads of the upper and wealthy classes in such form that they could be, so to speak, utilised as a room within a room, the framework of the bedstead being further assisted by hangings. The luxury of the age thus resulted in the making of a great amount of splendid structures, which were so much prized that they were frequently left as heirlooms or specially mentioned in wills and bequests. There is little wonder that their possessors should desire to place the acquirement of such precious articles on record. Oak bedsteads bearing seventeenth-century dates not infrequently find their way into present-day sale-rooms, and generally command high prices, though appreciation of them is not invariably shown. In April, 1908, a fine specimen, carved with caryatids, foliage, and strapwork, bearing the date of 1634, was knocked down for no more than fifty-five guineas at Messrs. Christie, Manson and Woods'. Several specimens of dated bedsteads and cradles remain in the National Collection at South Kensington, but it is to be feared that some of them have not altogether escaped the hands of the restorer.* The cradle illustrated in Plate LXV., an excellent specimen of such pieces in use among middle-class families, bears the following interesting inscription :—

14th DAI October C.M.B. 1641.

Though this cradle is in fine condition, the rockers are much worn, as if with constant use.

Besides boxes, chairs, cupboards, and bedsteads, implements and household utensils were frequently carved with the years in which they were constructed. In 1904 a very interesting discovery was made among some lumber in the Cambridge Corn Exchange, where an ancient standard bushel measure was unearthed, which, on examination, was found to be inscribed with the following words :—

ELIZABETH DEI GRACIA ANGLIÆ FRANCIÆ ET HIBERNIÆ
REGINA,

accompanied by the date 1601. Porringers and wooden platters inscribed with dates are also at times discovered, though rarely, in remote districts.

Examples of furniture occasionally crop up on which the dates, originally genuine, have been altered or falsified in order to give a spurious value to such pieces. The "Kroger" chest in the Victoria and Albert Museum, on which the date has been transformed from 1803 to 1603, is a case in point, and has been dealt with

---

* One bedstead, with finely moulded pillar-caps and inlaid panels at the back, is dated 1593.

in the author's work, *Old Oak Furniture;* but another piece, also at South Kensington, is not so well known, and seems to have escaped remark. The latter is an arm-chair of ash, from Vierlande, in Germany (No. 1113—1904), with turned spindle supports to the back and arms, and bearing on the back panel a carved rose and the incised inscription :—

SOPHIA WULFFS

ANNO 1795.

The date, on examination, will be found to be in part an alteration, probably from 1825, in a presumable endeavour to delude on the part of its one-time owners.

In conclusion to this chapter, let it be said that dates have been, and still are, added and affixed to furniture and fittings of old buildings, not only of the approximate periods to which such examples belong, but also in most appallingly loose and incorrect ways. The characteristic Jacobean screen at Apethorpe Hall, Northants., exhibits on one of its panels the inscription :—

VIRTVS SVPER OMNIA VINCAT 1364,

being only antedated by some 250 or 300 years.

The belfry ladder at Playden Church, Sussex, also shows an eleventh-century date, carved many years ago, but in *Arabic characters.* The spurious attribute on the Great Bed of Ware (*temp*. Elizabeth) has been dealt with in my book on *Old Oak Furniture,* and is of a character very different from the genuine date of the same epoch, with its cross-legged fours, which figures above the entry to the churchyard at Bray.

PLATE VIII.

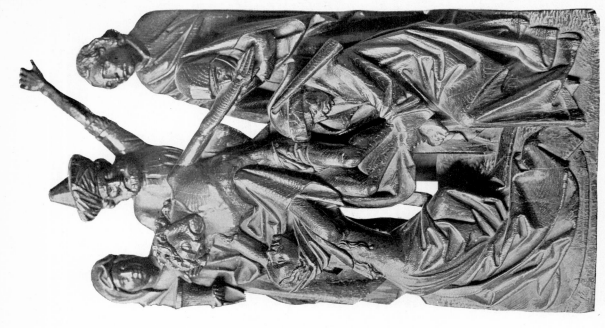

THE DESCENT FROM THE CROSS.   FRENCH OR FLEMISH.
FIFTEENTH CENTURY.

TRAVELLING TINKER (?).   CONTINENTAL.
END OF FIFTEENTH CENTURY.

Oak Carvings from the late Sir Edward Holden's Collection.

THE ENTOMBMENT.   FRENCH OR FLEMISH.
FIFTEENTH CENTURY.

CHAPTER IX.

Personal Experiences.

THAT this chapter could easily be extended to equal length with the rest of the book I have not the slightest doubt, and that it would not even then be the most wearisome portion I have also some views upon. But to be egotistical is a heinous fault to be accused of, and I will curtail these personal experiences—for this time at least. A good many adventures have been forgotten, but I shall hardly forget my first attempt to acquire a Gothic *meuble*. A youth affected with a singular passion for the pointed styles, I walked one April day, many years ago, into the Rue Eau de Robec in Rouen, in those days a veritable scrap depository of crazy odds and ends of furniture. The little bridges across the dirty ditch led straight up to dark, cavernous doorways in the old houses on the other side, contrasting sharply with the bright sunlight without. Inside one of these doorways, and half-obscured in shadow, stood a tall press, or armoire, in which a number of flamboyant panels were discernible. I crossed the bridge and endeavoured to examine the cupboard, which was half-covered with a litter of various descriptions. Yes! the panels were of fifteenth-century flamboyant design, bearing the arms of France and Brittany on shields inserted among the tracery. Very much worn and rubbed they appeared, a great deal more so than the framing, which suggested replacement of a later date, but the whole piece was covered with a coat of dark-brown paint, obscuring the outer surface. Inside everything was conformable: the backs of the panels presenting a semblance of decay, while the stiles and transoms showed up more sharply cut and of newer surface. The proprietor made his appearance, and things began to look interesting.

Monsieur was regarding the *meuble Gothique*. It was *tres belle pièce*, and very rare. The panels had been found in the Robec—which might account for their condition—the framing had been restored, but the piece was so very exceptional. The price was somewhere about five or six pounds, and I inwardly resolved that even if the framework was modern, the panels were well worth the money. But somehow the thing lingered. Were there any more such pieces? The proprietor would go and see. Left alone for a few minutes, something prompted me to scratch the face of one of the panels with my knife, and the bald truth was at once revealed. The beautiful flamboyant carvings were " squeezes" only, backed with old oak and painted on their fronts.

I did not acquire that armoire, though within a few hours I was lucky enough to get hold of some really genuine panels of similar character, and at a price which the present-day collector might search for in vain.

If you meet a hunting-man who asserts that he has never been thrown, don't believe him; similarly, if you are told by a collector that he has never once been taken in—well, you can say or think pretty much what you like about that person, whoever he may happen to be. The accounts of many subsequent failures to discriminate shall be passed over here.

Belief is pretty general amongst amateurs that " finds " in the raw and untouched state are verging on extinction, so swept is the countryside for business purposes nowadays; but for those who have eyes to see and ears to hear, some very attractive discoveries yet remain to be gathered in by the true collector. Quite recently, while exploring that part of the Thames haven which Mr. Arthur Morrison, the novelist, has made so alluring and so peculiarly his own, I chanced across a humble and rather lonely cottage, which displayed a modest announcement as to the supplying of tea and hot water. On the little grass-plot in front of the dwelling were gathered together some three or four tables and a few chairs, intended for the use of such festive parties as happened to find their way to this quiet and secluded spot. The tables were of different shapes and sizes, mainly of the commonest order, all painted a blatant white, and the tops alike covered with American cloth; but there was no mistaking the Carolean outline of one of them, with its pillar legs and moulded rails. The latter table, which had evidently been out in the weather for many years, had lost the best part of its feet through damp-rot, and had been elevated on splints of firewood in a very quaint manner; but it was of oak, and possessed a very elegant outline. An approach in due form was necessary. The owner of the establishment was engaged in thinning the hedges on his plot, and was summoned by his wife, who refused to do anything without the sanction of her better half. My enquiry elicited the information that the male vendor of refreshments would cheerfully sell the table for 2s. in order to replace it with a new one. I paid an inclusive sum to cover transport, and was asked doubtfully if I cared for such old stuff. An affirmative answer produced an old pistol from the man's pockets. " I've seen this kickin' about in the hedge for weeks, but it's no use to me. You can have it for sixpence." So that little silver-mounted pocket " barker," engraved with the monogram " J. J.," had evidently lain concealed among the hedge-roots ever since some desperate affray or smuggling raid early in the nineteenth century. What lost histories are those of the Carolean table and hidden Georgian pistol, and what fresh imaginative romances could be weaved around them!

In 1910, while sojourning at a town in Northern France, I detected some interesting looking antiquities in an establishment connected with carriage hiring. The articles were obviously *à vendre*, but the assistant could not give me any information except that the proprietor was out at the time, and that he had gone to view a Gothic armoire, which was said to have come from the crypt of the old church. This sounded interesting. An appointment was arranged for the afternoon, and my second visit unearthed *M. le Propriétaire*, one of the handsomest and finest men it has ever been my luck to set eyes on. I purchased a few things of no great account, and then made enquiries as to the mysterious *meuble Gothique*. It appeared that the individual who owned the piece was uncertain as to his habits, but my magnificent Frenchman would take me to the place where it remained. A short walk brought us to a neat old-fashioned house in a sunny square. No answer was returned to repeated applications at the door, but a neighbour who appeared volunteered the information that though the resident had been called away on business, she could take us inside. The hall and front room were partly filled up with two or three heavy, uninteresting armoires or presses, dating possibly from the reign of Louis XIV., and not remarkably desirable from the collector's point of view. My conductor interrogated the woman who had let us into the house, and then made his way to a room at the back. I have no notion as to whether he expected me to accompany him, but I went, and to my surprise entered a very complete "faker's" workshop. Amidst the tools and pickling stuffs were the dismantled sections of another ponderous Louis cupboard, which was in process of transition into a *pièce Gothique*. It was all very interesting. Such proceedings are a pity, but there was so much superfluous material in this case to work upon that no great amount of harm was done—certainly not to me!

It is not many collectors who have the good fortune to bring home veritable specimens of Gothic art after a day's casual outing in the country, but it has fallen to my lot several times, and always in the most unexpected manner. One Saturday, a few years ago, I visited a little town in the Eastern Counties, where communication with London was difficult and unsatisfactory. Trains were but few, and the connections were irritating, not to say thoroughly bad. I had tea at a cosy old-fashioned inn, after inspecting everything that was interesting in the place, and was preparing to return when I ran across a small general shop which had hitherto escaped my notice. In the window a very indifferent chest of "Charley" type was exhibited among a scanty display of curios, but what interested me most was the sight of an undoubted fifteenth-century joint-stool, which was standing in a lop-sided fashion among some lumber down the adjacent yard. The good woman who answered my summons was very morose; she could not tell me the price of anything, as her husband had gone out, and they had disagreed about some sales she had effected. She refused to name a price for the stool or anything else until her husband came back, which I suspected would be from the nearest public-house. When he would return she did not know, and she would do absolutely nothing without the man. There was no help for it, waiting was my only chance. I went all over the town again, and finally returned to the inn for some supper. The last train for London left between nine and ten, and this would land me home at something past midnight, but I was determined to have that stool if possible. The little private room at the inn was illuminated by a very insufficient oil-lamp, and I sat and ate cold meat and read a weird book of occult stories till time was nearly up. Arriving once more at the shop, it was at once apparent, from a wordy warfare going on, that the owner had returned in a heated and argumentative condition. He had not intended to sell the stool, but I could have it for five shillings, and he would carry it to the railway station for me if I would give him the price of a drink. Payment was duly made and accepted, and we started, accompanied by some flowers of speech from the woman as a send-off. On the way my man, who took matters in what seemed to me a very leisurely way, displayed a remarkable disposition to rest and tell me all about his family quarrels. The whistle sounded as we arrived outside the railway station. There was no time to get a ticket; my precious stool was bundled into a ramshackle carriage as the train was moving, and I fell in after it, the only passenger, tired out but successful.

PLATE IX.

TYPES OF CONSTRUCTION

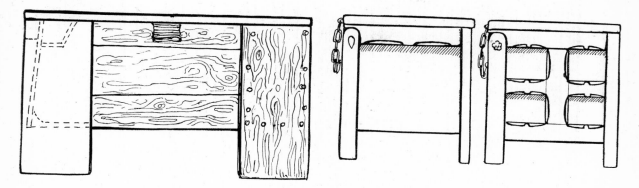

Type I.—The thirteenth-century coffer, front and ends.

Type II.—The fourteenth-century coffer, with simulated panelling.

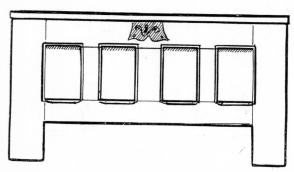

Type III.—The panelled chest, with heavy framing.

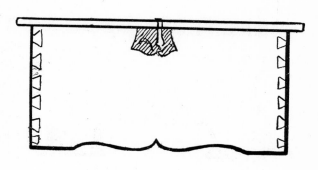

Type IV.—The coffer with dovetailed edges.

E

PLATE X.

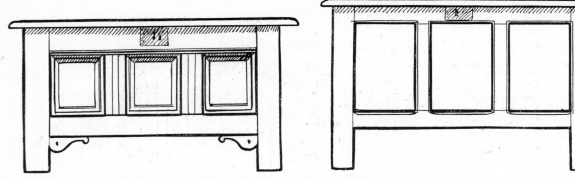

TYPE V.—ELIZABETHAN CHEST.   TYPE VI.—JACOBEAN CHEST.

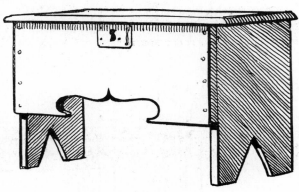

TYPE VII.—THE SLAB-ENDED BOX.

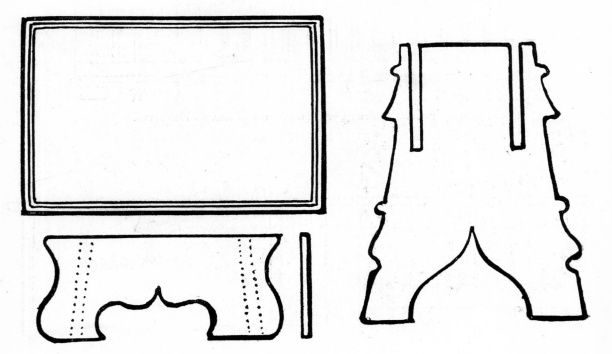

CONSTRUCTION OF GOTHIC STOOL.

PLATE XI.

PERIOD FURNITURE

LATE TWELFTH-CENTURY COFFER, IN HINDRINGHAM CHURCH, NORFOLK.

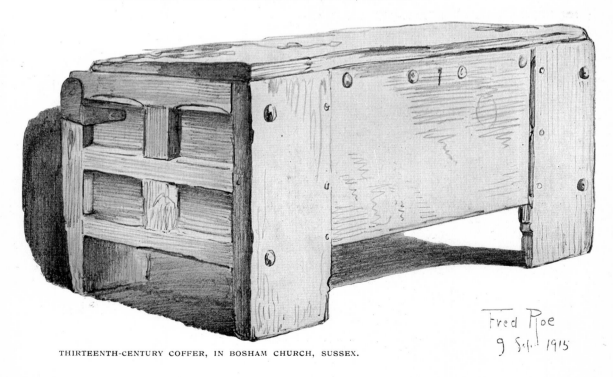

THIRTEENTH-CENTURY COFFER, IN BOSHAM CHURCH, SUSSEX.

PLATE XII.

PANEL FROM A THIRTEENTH-CENTURY COFFRET.   IN SAFFRON WALDEN MUSEUM.

FOOT OF THE BOSHAM COFFER.

PLATE XIII.

LATE FOURTEENTH-CENTURY COFFER, IN YORK CATHEDRAL.

COFFER OF THE PERPENDICULAR PERIOD, FORMERLY IN SEDLESCOMBE CHURCH, SUSSEX.
FROM A SKETCH BY REV. E. GODDARD, 1835 (T. H. HORSFIELD'S "COUNTY OF SUSSEX").

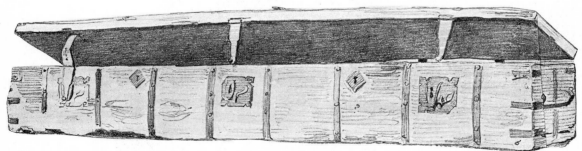

LATE FOURTEENTH OR EARLY FIFTEENTH-CENTURY COFFER, IN CHICHESTER CATHEDRAL.
LENGTH, 8 FT. 8 IN.; WIDTH, 16 IN.; DEPTH, 16 IN.

F

PLATE XIV.

FOURTEENTH-CENTURY COFFRET (NOW IN POSSESSION
OF THE MARQUIS OF GRANBY); AND A CHEST, WITH
PARCHEMIN PANELS, EARLY SIXTEENTH CENTURY.

FOURTEENTH-CENTURY BUTTRESSED COFFER, IN
ST. JOHN'S HOSPITAL, CANTERBURY.

THE CRADLE OF HENRY V., NOW IN THE LONDON MUSEUM.

PLATE XV.

FOURTEENTH-CENTURY COFFER, IN BRANCEPETH CHURCH, NORTHUMBERLAND.
FROM A DRAWING BY MR. W. G. FOOTITT.

LATE FOURTEENTH-CENTURY BOX. WESTPHALIAN. IN THE POSSESSION OF MR. F. GORDON ROE.
THE STRAPS AND IRONWORK GENERALLY ARE TYPICAL OF THE PERIOD. THE TERMINATIONS OF
THE HANDLE ARE FORMED AS BOARS' HEADS.

PLATE XVI.

FIFTEENTH-CENTURY PANEL. A RELIC OF THE CHOIR-FITTINGS OF
YORK CATHEDRAL. SALVED FROM THE FIRE OCCASIONED BY THE
INCENDIARY MARTIN IN 1829. AUTHOR'S COLLECTION.

PLATE XVII.

EARLY SIXTEENTH-CENTURY SIDE-TABLE,   VICTORIA AND ALBERT MUSEUM.

SIXTEENTH-CENTURY DRAW-TABLE AND BENCH, FROM BROADWAY, NEAR ILMINSTER, SOMERSET.
VICTORIA AND ALBERT MUSEUM.

PLATE XVIII.

FIFTEENTH-CENTURY CHEST.   FRENCH.   FROM THE COLLECTION OF THE LATE BARON SWINFEN OF CHERTSEY.

LATE FIFTEENTH CENTURY CUPBOARD.   VICTORIA AND ALBERT MUSEUM.

PLATE XIX.

EARLY SIXTEENTH-CENTURY DOLE-CUPBOARD, SAID TO HAVE COME FROM IVY CHURCH, AN OLD HOUSE AT
ALDERBURY, NEAR SALISBURY, FORMERLY A MONASTERY, NOW IN RUINS. VICTORIA AND ALBERT MUSEUM.

CHEST. FIRST HALF OF SIXTEENTH CENTURY. WESTPHALIAN.
THE TRAY OF THIS CHEST HAS A SMALL SECRET PLACE IN A DOUBLE BOTTOM.

PLATE XX.

LATE FIFTEENTH OR EARLY SIXTEENTH-CENTURY CABINET.
FOUND IN A BARN OF AN OLD MANOR-HOUSE NEAR BRADFIELD, SHEFFIELD.

BOX OF WOOD, COVERED WITH "CUIR-BOUILLI," BOUND WITH IRON STRAPS.
PRESENTED TO LINCOLN'S INN IN 1549 BY ITS THEN TREASURER, HENRY HEYDON.

PLATE XXI.

EXAMPLES OF TYROLESE FURNITURE OF GOTHIC DESIGN, AND A FRENCH OR FLEMISH CHEST
CARVED WITH FLEURS-DE-LYS.

PLATE XXII.

TWO TYROLESE GOTHIC CUPBOARDS.   MUNICH NATIONAL MUSEUM.

PLATE XXIII.

LATE GOTHIC COFFER.   TEMP. HENRY VII. OR HENRY VIII.
THE "HERRING-BONE" PATTERN IS TYPICAL OF THIS PERIOD; THE ROUNDED TOPS TO THE TRACERY ARE
ALSO INDICATIVE; BOTH FEATURES WERE TO BE FOUND IN WOODWORK AT THE DAWN OF THE RENAISSANCE.

LATE GOTHIC COFFER, IN THAXTED CHURCH, ESSEX.
THE METHOD OF CONSTRUCTION WITH SLAB ENDS, THE LATE OGEE ARCHES, AND THE STRING-COURSES
WITHOUT TERMINATIONS, ARE CHARACTERISTIC.

PLATE XXIV.

CHEST. TEMP. HENRY VIII. IN THE POSSESSION OF COL. H. C. T. LITTLEDALE.
THE CARVING ON THE PANELS IS COMPARABLE WITH THAT AT ABINGTON ABBEY, NORTHANTS. SEE PLATE XXXIV.

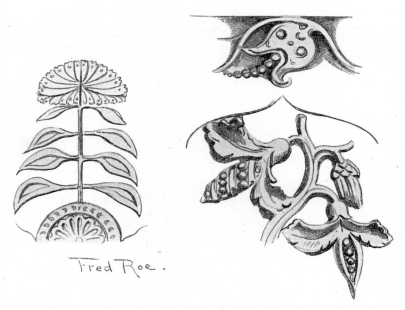

TYPES OF TUDOR FLOWERING FOUND ON FURNITURE OF THE PERIOD.

PLATE XXV.

CHAIR TABLE, END OF FIFTEENTH CENTURY.
A PROGENITOR OF THE OFTEN MISNAMED "MONK'S BENCH."
IN THE AUTHOR'S COLLECTION.

Fred Roe

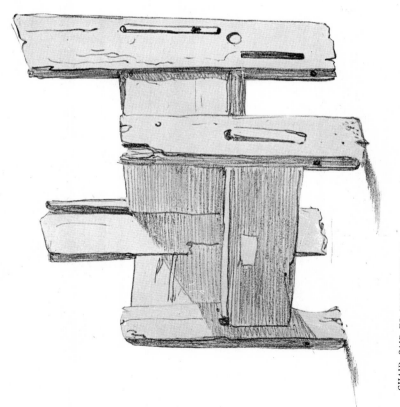

CHAIR SAID TO HAVE BEEN USED BY ST. AUGUSTINE AT HIS CONFERENCE
WITH THE BRITISH BISHOPS AT AUGUSTINE'S OAK.
FORMERLY IN STAUNTON CHURCH; NOW IN CANTERBURY MUSEUM.
ACTUAL AGE PROBLEMATICAL; PERHAPS DATING FROM FIFTEENTH CENTURY.

PLATE XXVI.

GOTHIC JOINT STOOL, IN BREDE CHURCH, SUSSEX.

FIFTEENTH-CENTURY COFFRET.
FROM THE LATE WALTER WITHALL'S COLLECTION.

PLATE XXVII.

JOINT STOOL, IN SAFFRON WALDEN MUSEUM.

FRONT PANEL IN, THE ANCIENT CORPORATION COFFER FORMERLY KEPT IN THE MOOT HALL, IPSWICH, AND
NOW IN CHRISTCHURCH MANSION, IPSWICH.   MEASUREMENTS OF PANEL, $19\frac{1}{2}$ IN. BY $52\frac{1}{2}$ IN.

PLATE XXVIII.

GAMING TABLE, 1530, IN THE POSSESSION OF LORD DE L'ISLE.
THIS IS, PRESUMABLY, THE SPECIMEN ILLUSTRATED IN SHAW'S "SPECIMENS OF
ANCIENT FURNITURE," WHICH DESCRIBES IT AS BEING THEN AT HILL HALL, ESSEX.

GOTHIC JOINT STOOL.   IN POSSESSION OF
THE MARQUESS OF GRANBY.

JOINT STOOL.   FROM A FIFTEENTH-CENTURY "BOOK
OF HOURS," BODLEIAN LIBRARY (MS. CANON LIT., 99).

PLATE XXIX.

"GRACE BEFORE MEAT," BY JAN STEEN.   AT BELVOIR CASTLE.
THIS INTERESTING PICTURE SHOWS A LINEN-PANELLED CUPBOARD-SEAT, OF A DATE ANTERIOR TO THE PAINTING.
IT IS A VERY FAITHFUL REPRESENTATION OF THE USE OF SUCH BEAUTIFUL PIECES.

G

PLATE XXX.

MIDDLE OF THE SIXTEENTH-CENTURY CHEST FRONT. THE ROUNDELS, HEADS, AND ARABESQUES
INDICATE STRONGLY THE INFLUENCE OF THE ITALIAN RENAISSANCE UPON FLEMISH CARVING OF THE PERIOD.

LINEN-PANELLED CHEST, WITH LIGHT FRAMING. FRENCH OR FLEMISH. EARLY SIXTEENTH CENTURY.
THE THINNESS OF THE STILES INDICATES A LATE PERIOD OF GOTHIC ART.

PLATE XXXI.

FIFTEENTH-CENTURY PANELS.   FRENCH, FROM ROUEN.   SIXTEENTH-CENTURY PANEL.   RHONE VALLEY OR THE SAVOY.
IN THE AUTHOR'S COLLECTION.

PLATE XXXII.

MID-SIXTEENTH-CENTURY PANEL.   NORTHERN FRENCH OR FLEMISH.   AUTHOR'S COLLECTION.

PLATE XXXIII.

FRENCH CREDENCE OF RENAISSANCE DESIGN.   IN THE COLLECTION OF MR. ERNEST WYTHES.

PLATE XXXIV.

PRIOR THOMAS SILKSTED'S COFFER, DATED 1519, IN SHANKLIN CHURCH, ISLE OF WIGHT.
FROM SHAW'S "SPECIMENS OF ANCIENT FURNITURE."

JONGLEURS CARVED ON THE FRIEZE OF A ROOM, AT ABINGTON ABBEY, NORTHANTS.
TEMP. HENRY VIII.

PLATE XXXV.

THIS BEAUTIFUL SPECIMEN OF A TUDOR COURT CUPBOARD CAME FROM OTFORD, IN KENT, WHERE IT WAS DISCOVERED IN AN OUT-HOUSE DOING DUTY AS A RECEPTACLE FOR CHEESES. COLLECTION OF SIR EDWARD BARRY, BART.

PLATE XXXVI.

PANEL. TEMP. HENRY VIII.
FROM THE WALTHAM ABBEY
ROOM. VICTORIA AND ALBERT
MUSEUM.

DOOR, WALNUT. SOUTHERN
FRENCH, 1526. VICTORIA
AND ALBERT MUSEUM.

THE "JESTER" PANEL, AT RYE HOUSE. TEMP. HENRY VIII.
ONE OF THE FEW AUTHENTIC REPRESENTATIONS IN WOOD OF
A JESTER; ANOTHER BEING ON SOME FRENCH PANELLING, A
CAST OF WHICH IS AT SOUTH KENSINGTON.
IN EACH CASE HUMOROUS EXPRESSIONS ARE INDICATED.

PLATE XXXVII.

CHEST FRONT.   FRENCH, TEMP. FRANÇOIS IER.   IN THE AUTHOR'S COLLECTION.

CUPBOARD, ILLUSTRATING THE DECADENCE OF THE LINEN PANEL.
IN THE POSSESSION OF MR. T. C. PARKER.

PLATE XXXVIII.

SIXTEENTH-CENTURY CASSONE. WALNUT. ITALIAN.

SIXTEENTH-CENTURY CASSONE. WALNUT. ITALIAN. FROM THE SOULAGES COLLECTION.
VICTORIA AND ALBERT MUSEUM.

PLATE XXXIX.

SIXTEENTH-CENTURY STATE CHAIR.   FRENCH.
VICTORIA AND ALBERT MUSEUM.

STATE CHAIR.   FRENCH (LYONS).
FROM THE PIERPONT MORGAN COLLECTION.
FORMERLY IN THE ROUGIER COLLECTION.

PLATE XL.

SIXTEENTH-CENTURY BUFFET, AT FONTAINEBLEAU.   FRENCH.

PLATE XLI.

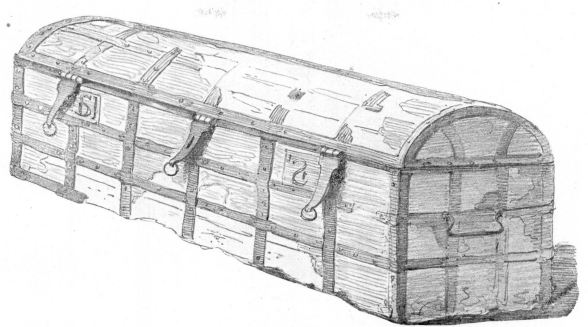

IRON-BOUND COFFER.   PROBABLY LATE SIXTEENTH CENTURY.   DISCOVERED IN A SECRET HIDING-PLACE
AT INGATESTONE HALL, ESSEX, AND ALLUDED TO BY MISS BRADDON IN "LADY AUDLEY'S SECRET."

SIXTEENTH-CENTURY IRON-BOUND COFFER, IN FRAMLINGHAM CHURCH, SUFFOLK.

PLATE XLII.

SIXTEENTH-CENTURY IRON-BOUND COFFER.
AT ST. SWITHIN'S CHURCH, WORCESTER.

IRON-BOUND COFFER.   REPLACING ONE BROKEN INTO IN 1590.
AT WEST GATE, WINCHESTER.

PLATE XLIII.

ALMS-BOX, DATED 1589.   IN DOVERCOURT CHURCH, ESSEX.

PLATE XLIV.

SECRETAIRE, DATED 1594.   THE UPPER PORTION IS OF CAMPHOR OR CYPRESS-
WOOD, AND IS OF ITALIAN ORIGIN.   THESE SECRETAIRES WERE OFTEN PROVIDED
WITH A SUBSTRUCTURE OF OAK UPON THEIR IMPORTATION INTO ENGLAND, AS IN THE
SPECIMEN SHOWN.   AUTHOR'S COLLECTION.

PLATE XLV.

ATLAS ON CHEST. DATED 1639. FROM THE LATE SIR CHARLES LAWES-WITTERONGE'S COLLECTION.

SIXTEENTH-CENTURY DESK, IN THE POSSESSION OF MR. T. C. PARKER.

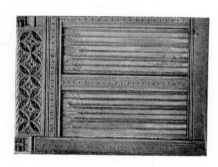

LINEN-PANELS.

SIXTEENTH-CENTURY PANEL OF THE GROTESQUE TYPE PREVAILING AT THIS PERIOD.

H

PLATE XLVI.

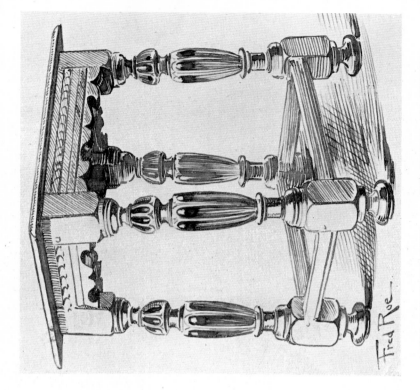

A FINE ELIZABETHAN STOOL.   THE GROOVED AND JEWELLED
LEGS DISPLAY SUPERIOR WORKMANSHIP, TYPICAL OF THE TIME.

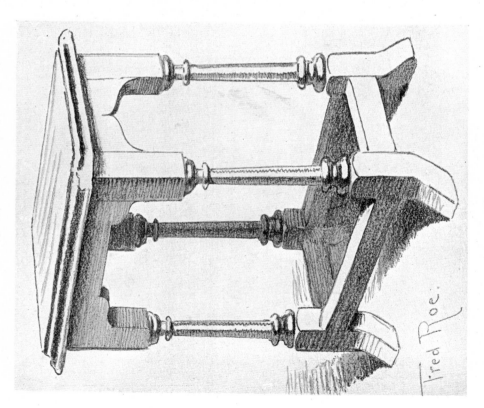

COFFIN STOOL, IN GREAT BRAXTED CHURCH, ESSEX.

PLATE XLVII.

THE GREAT HALL, PENSHURST, SHOWING THE "INDEPENDENT TOPPED" TABLES SPECIALLY MADE FOR THIS
POSITION IN TUDOR TIMES.   JAMES I. AND CHARLES I. (THEN PRINCE) WERE ENTERTAINED AT PENSHURST,
AND THESE TABLES WERE DOUBTLESS IN PLACE AT THE TIME OF THE EVENT.

PLATE XLVIII.

ELIZABETHAN DRAW-TABLE; A VERY BEAUTIFUL SPECIMEN IN FINE CONDITION, RICHLY INLAID WITH HOLLY AND BOG-OAK ON ITS STRETCHERS.   VICTORIA AND ALBERT MUSEUM.

EIGHT-LEGGED TABLES OF THE SIXTEENTH CENTURY ARE EXCEEDINGLY SCARCE.

PLATE XLIX.

DRAW-TABLE OF UNUSUAL FORM.   FIRST QUARTER OF SEVENTEENTH CENTURY.

ELIZABETHAN DRAW-TABLE.

SEVENTEENTH-CENTURY DRAW-TABLE.   DUTCH.   IN POSSESSION OF MR. ARTHUR L. RADFORD.

PLATE L.

APETHORPE HALL, NORTHANTS, SHOWING THE SPURIOUS "1364" DATE ON THE SCREEN, AND TABLES OF A SOMEWHAT
LATER PERIOD THAN THOSE AT PENSHURST.

PLATE LI.

ELIZABETHAN PANELLING OF THE "NELSON ROOM," STAR HOTEL, GREAT YARMOUTH.

NAME INSCRIBED ON A SEVENTEENTH-CENTURY TABLE IN THE POSSESSION OF
MR. RICHARD H. MORTEN, THE SAVOY, DENHAM, BUCKS.   THE INSTONES WERE
A YEOMAN FAMILY RESIDING IN THE NEIGHBOURHOOD DURING THE SEVENTEENTH
CENTURY, THEIR DESCENDANTS DISPOSING OF THE TABLE *circa* 1863.

PLATE LII.

DETAILS OF AN ELIZABETHAN BEDSTEAD, FROM THE COLLECTION OF THE LATE SIR EDWARD HOLDEN, BART.

PLATE LIII.

BEDSTEAD-HEAD.   YORKSHIRE.   FIRST HALF OF SEVENTEENTH CENTURY.

ELIZABETHAN CHEST.   IN THE POSSESSION OF MR. L. WALFORD, OF BUDLEIGH SALTERTON.

PLATE LIV.

SIXTEENTH-CENTURY TABLE, SUTTON PLACE, SURREY.

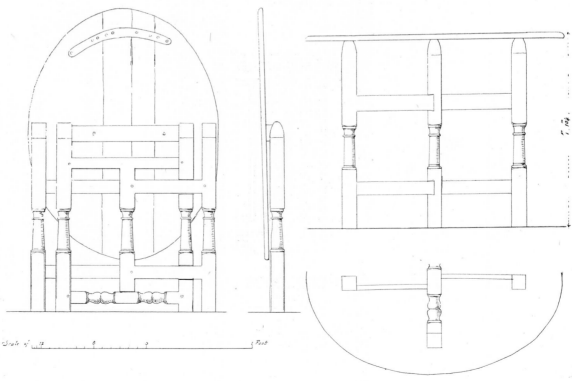

SEVENTEENTH-CENTURY TRAVELLING TABLE.   IN THE AUTHOR'S COLLECTION.

PLATE LV.

SEVENTEENTH CENTURY FIREPLACE, IN CATHERINE OF
ARAGON'S HOUSE, SHREWSBURY.

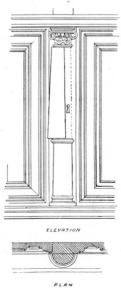

ELEVATION

PLAN

MECHANISM OF MOVABLE PILLAR HIDING KEYHOLE OF
DUTCH CABINET.   THE SHAFT OF THE PILLAR IS EBONISED.
SEE PLATE LVI.

PLATE LVI.

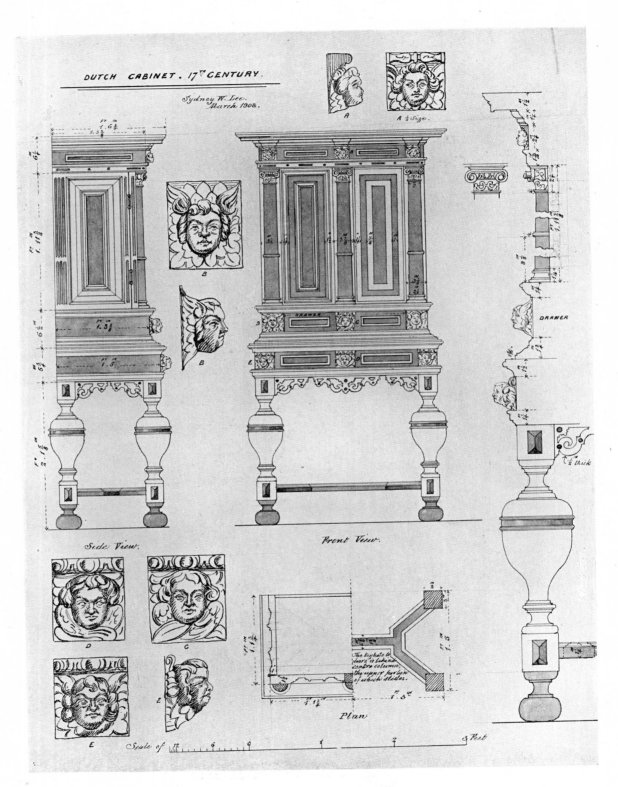

DUTCH CABINET. 17ᵀᴴ CENTURY.

Sydney W. Lee.
March 1908.

Side View.

Front View.

Plan

Scale of

SEVENTEENTH-CENTURY CABINET.   DUTCH.   IN THE AUTHOR'S COLLECTION.

PLATE LVII.

TWO CHAIRS.   TEMP. CHARLES I. AND ELIZABETH.   THE EARLIER CAME FROM RICHMOND, YORKS,
AND BEARS THE INITIALS OF WILLIAM BLAND, WHO FLOURISHED IN THE REIGNS OF MARY AND ELIZABETH.
AUTHOR'S COLLECTION.

DUG-OUT COFFER, IN BISHOP'S CLEEVE CHURCH, GLOUCESTER.
THE LOCKS SUGGEST FOURTEENTH OR FIFTEENTH-CENTURY WORK, WHICH IS
THE ONLY INDICATION OF AGE.

PLATE LVIII.

TWO INTERESTING BIBLE-BOXES, IN MR. TOWNROE'S COLLECTION. THAT CARVED WITH THE GUILLOCHE
AND ROSE PATTERN IS JACOBEAN. THE OTHER IS RARER, SINCE IT BEARS THE COMMONWEALTH DATE
OF 1652. THE LITTLE MASK UNDER THE LOCK-PLATE IS INTENDED TO REPRESENT CHARLES I., SHOWING
THE ORIGINAL OWNER OF THE BOX TO HAVE HAD ROYALIST SYMPATHIES. SUCH MASKS ARE SELDOM
FOUND ON BIBLE-BOXES; THEY OCCUR USUALLY ON THE SO-CALLED "YORKSHIRE" TALL-BACKED CHAIRS, AND
ON THE HILTS OF "MORTUARY" SWORDS.

PLATE LIX.

CHAIR, DATED 1649. VICTORIA AND ALBERT MUSEUM.

BIBLE-BOX. FIRST HALF OF SEVENTEENTH CENTURY. FROM COLCHESTER.
IN THE POSSESSION OF MR. F. GORDON ROE.

PLATE LX.

SEVENTEENTH-CENTURY CHEST.   BORDERS OF OXON AND WARWICK.
POSSIBLY OF SCOTTISH ORIGIN.

LATE SIXTEENTH OR EARLY SEVENTEENTH-CENTURY CHEST.

PLATE LXI.

FLEMISH CUPBOARD.   SEVENTEENTH CENTURY.
THIS IS A TYPICAL SPECIMEN OF THE DUTCH RENAISSANCE ; MANY SIMILAR SPECIMENS.
HAVE BEEN ATTRIBUTED ERRONEOUSLY TO OUR ELIZABETHAN CRAFTSMEN.
VICTORIA AND ALBERT MUSEUM.

I

PLATE LXII.

SPOON-CUPBOARD AND KNIFE-BOX, JUNCTION OF THE SEVENTEENTH AND EIGHTEENTH CENTURIES.
AN INTERESTING SPECIMEN FOR PURELY DOMESTIC USE.   AUTHOR'S COLLECTION.

PLATE LXIII.

LATE SIXTEENTH OR EARLY SEVENTEENTH-CENTURY CHEST, FORMERLY IN WINTERBOURNE HOUSE, NEAR BRISTOL.

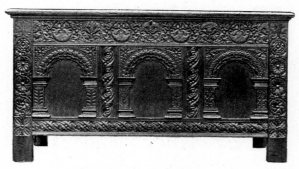

FIRST HALF OF THE SEVENTEENTH CENTURY.   WEST SOMERSET.

JACOBEAN CHEST, FROM CHURCH STRETTON, SHROPSHIRE.

PLATE LXIV.

SEVENTEENTH-CENTURY MARQUETERIE CHEST.   FROM MADAME BLANCHE MARCHESI'S COLLECTION.

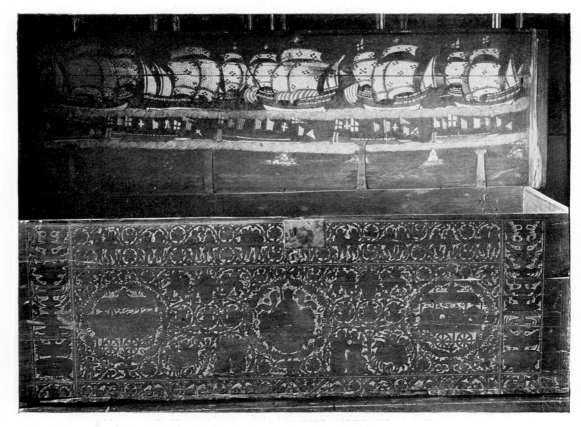

RED CEDAR-WOOD COFFER, WITH PAINTED LID.   ITALIAN.   EARLY SIXTEENTH CENTURY.

PLATE LXV.

SETTLE. SEVENTEENTH CENTURY. DISCOVERED IN A PUBLIC-HOUSE AT RIPPONDEN,
ON THE BORDERS OF YORKS. AND LANCS.

CRADLE, DATED 1641. VICTORIA AND ALBERT MUSEUM.

PLATE LXVI.

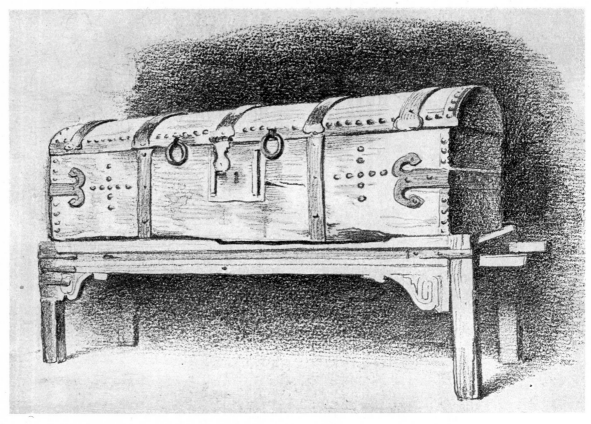

COFFER, IN FINGRINGHOE CHURCH, ESSEX.   THE DATE (1684) IS PROBABLY AN ADDITION.

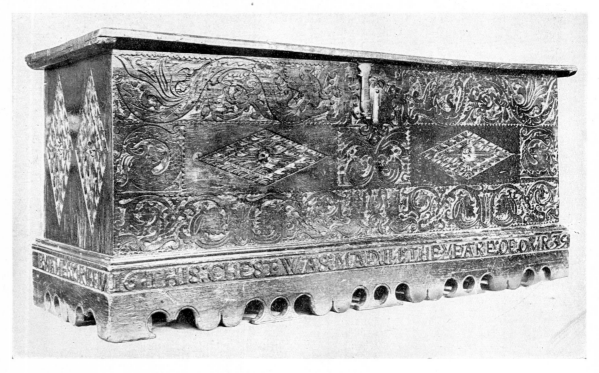

COFFER, MADE BY JAMES GRIFFIN IN 1639.   VICTORIA AND ALBERT MUSEUM.

PLATE LXVII.

LATE SIXTEENTH OR EARLY SEVENTEENTH-CENTURY SLAB-END COFFER, WITH INCISED DECORATION. ELM.
THE BORDURE OF TRAILED CONVENTIONAL ROSE-LEAVES IS UNCOMMON, AND REMINISCENT OF EARLIER TIMES.

TYROLESE CHEST, DATED 1624. PINEWOOD. IN THE COLLECTION OF MAJOR-GENERAL SIR COLERIDGE
GROVE, K.C.B. THIS TYPICAL SPECIMEN EXHIBITS SURVIVAL OF GOTHIC INFLUENCE.

PLATE LXVIII.

Fred Roe

CHEST OF DRAWERS. SECOND HALF OF SEVENTEENTH CENTURY. EASTERN COUNTIES.
AUTHOR'S COLLECTION.

PLATE LXIX.

SPICE CUPBOARD.   SECOND HALF OF THE SEVENTEENTH CENTURY.   AUTHOR'S COLLECTION.

CABINET, INLAID WITH MOTHER-O'-PEARL AND IVORY.
SECOND HALF OF THE SEVENTEENTH CENTURY.

PLATE LXX.

SMALL SQUARE JACOBEAN STOOL.   FROM POUND'S BRIDGE, KENT.
AUTHOR'S COLLECTION.

INSCRIPTION CARVED ON LID OF OAK COFFER, FORMERLY CONTAINING
DOCUMENTS OF THE FREE SCHOOL, AND NOW IN THE COURT HOUSE, RYE.

PLATE LXXI.

TRIANGULAR CHAIR, FORMERLY AT CHESHUNT
GREAT HOUSE.   ATTRIBUTED TO CARDINAL
WOLSEY.   ACTUALLY SEVENTEENTH CENTURY.

CAROLEAN STOOL.   KNOLE.

ARMCHAIR, INSCRIBED W.W., 1699.
FORMERLY IN COTE HOUSE, BRISTOL.

EARLY SEVENTEENTH-CENTURY CHAIR
FOUND IN CHELSEA.

PLATE LXXII.

CHAIR WITH PIERCED BACK. FLEMISH, SEVENTEENTH CENTURY. FROM THE LATE WALTER WITHALL'S COLLECTION.

CHAIR. TEMP. CHARLES II. FROM THE LATE SIR EDWARD HOLDEN'S COLLECTION.

PLATE LXXIII.

DAY-BED.   TEMP. CHARLES II.   FROM THE LATE SIR EDWARD HOLDEN'S COLLECTION.

PLATE LXXIV.

TWO CHAIRS FROM THE LATE SIR EDWARD HOLDEN'S COLLECTION.

TEMP. WILLIAM AND MARY.   LATE SEVENTEENTH CENTURY.

THE BELL-SHAPED MEMBERS ON THE LEGS OF THE ARMCHAIR ARE TYPICAL OF THE TIME.

PLATE LXXV.

STOOL, AT MIDHURST PARISH CHURCH, INSCRIBED

I — B
16   89
T — P

AND SHOWING A SURVIVAL OF THE GOTHIC FORM.

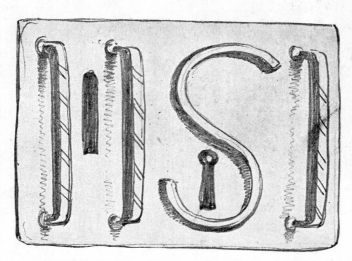

LOCK-PLATE ON THE INGATESTONE COFFER.   SEE PLATE XLI.
FROM BUCKLER'S "TWENTY-TWO CHURCHES OF ESSEX," 1856.

PLATE LXXVI.

DUTCH BOX.   SEVENTEENTH CENTURY.   IN THE POSSESSION OF MR. J. B. HARRIS-BURLAND.

CARVED WINDOW-SILL IN MAIDEN LANE, STAMFORD, SAVED FROM DESTRUCTION BY MR. H. F. TRAYLEN, F.R.I.B.A.
THE ARMORIAL BEARINGS ARE THOSE OF THE DIGBYS.   THIS SPECIMEN IS INCLUDED AS THE CARVING IS SO
EXCEEDINGLY TYPICAL OF THE FIFTEENTH-CENTURY CRAFTSMAN'S ART.